DailyOM

HAY HOUSE TITLES OF RELATED INTEREST

YOU CAN HEAL YOUR LIFE, the movie,
starring Louise L. Hay & Friends
(available as a 1-DVD program and an expanded 2-DVD set)
Watch the trailer at: **www.LouiseHayMovie.com**

THE SHIFT, the movie,
starring Dr. Wayne W. Dyer
(available as a 1-DVD program and an expanded 2-DVD set)
Watch the trailer at: **www.DyerMovie.com**

◆

*CHANGE YOUR THOUGHTS — CHANGE YOUR LIFE: Living
the Wisdom of the Tao,* by Dr. Wayne W. Dyer

*FINDING OUR WAY HOME:
Heartwarming Stories That Ignite Our Spiritual Core,*
by Gerald Jampolsky, M.D., and Diane Cirincione, Ph.D.

*HEALING WORDS FROM THE ANGELS:
365 Daily Messages,* by Doreen Virtue

*MANIFEST YOUR DESIRES: 365 Ways to Make
Your Dreams a Reality,* by Esther and Jerry Hicks
(The Teachings of Abraham®)

THE PRESENT MOMENT: 365 Daily Affirmations,
by Louise L. Hay

◆

All of the above are available at your
local bookstore, or may be ordered by visiting:

Hay House USA: **www.hayhouse.com**®
Hay House Australia: **www.hayhouse.com.au**
Hay House UK: **www.hayhouse.co.uk**
Hay House South Africa: **www.hayhouse.co.za**
Hay House India: **www.hayhouse.co.in**

DailyOM

INSPIRATIONAL THOUGHTS
FOR A HAPPY, HEALTHY,
AND FULFILLING DAY

MADISYN TAYLOR

HAY HOUSE, INC.

Carlsbad, California • New York City
London • Sydney • Johannesburg
Vancouver • Hong Kong • New Delhi

Published and distributed in the United States by: Hay House, Inc.: www.
hayhouse.com • *Published and distributed in Australia by:* Hay House Australia
Pty. Ltd.: www.hayhouse.com.au • *Published and distributed in the United
Kingdom by:* Hay House UK, Ltd.: www.hayhouse.co.uk • *Published and
distributed in the Republic of South Africa by:* Hay House SA (Pty), Ltd.: www.
hayhouse.co.za • *Distributed in Canada by:* Raincoast: www.raincoast.com •
Published in India by: Hay House Publishers India: www.hayhouse.co.in

Editorial supervision: Jill Kramer

Library of Congress Cataloging-in-Publication Data

Taylor, Madisyn.
 DailyOM : inspirational thoughts for a happy, healthy, and fulfilling day /
Madisyn Taylor. -- 1st ed.
  p. cm.
 ISBN 978-1-4019-2050-0 (tradepaper)
 1. Meditations. I. Title.
 BL624.2.T39 2008
 158.1'28--dc22

                                2007037772

ISBN: 978-1-4019-2050-0
Digital ISBN: 978-1-4019-2136-1

15 14 13 12   7 6 5 4
1st edition, April 2008
4th edition, February 2012

Printed in the United States of America

CONTENTS

INTRODUCTION

In 2004 I co-founded DailyOM with my husband with the vision of sending messages of hope, awareness, and love through e-mail. Every day we send stories on topics such as meditation, relationships, nature, as well as words that simply touch your heart. They are events and circumstances in life that we all go through as human beings on our path to growth.

Since the beginning of our journey, we have always wanted to put the wisdom of DailyOM in a book, and you are now holding the first volume in your hands. Allow the energy of the words within these pages to gently guide you on your path to awareness and self-fulfillment.

As editor-in-chief of DailyOM, I am often asked how I come up with story ideas every day. Indeed, this is one of the most difficult parts of my job—but then again, it can be the easiest as well. Most often the ideas are given to me in meditation, and sometimes the universe will have me look at my own life and write about my personal experiences. After all, we are all on the same earth together having very similar experiences. Nature is always a large part of my inspiration . . . and every day I am in awe of her beauty, wisdom, and willingness to help heal humanity.

We all experience joy, pain, love, and grief—none of us are immune, including me. I have walked the path just as all of you have, and I have examined my life in depth and made changes where I felt they were needed. I could not make these offerings to you without doing the work myself. It is my sincere hope that you can find comfort in these messages; that they perhaps spark a fire in you, create conversation, or bring about change; and even that you learn something new if you choose. I'm so happy to have you along on our journey.

Many blessings,
Madisyn

LINKING CENTER
CHECKING IN WITH YOUR HEART

Every day we experience a magical twilight between our dreaming and waking states. During this brief period of time, our minds still remember that all things are possible. We can smoothly transition into the physical world without losing a sense of hope when we first check in with our heart center before we even get out of bed.

Our heart center is the link between body and spirit, instinct and inspiration. It does not take long to hold a thought of loving gratitude for that which beats within us — in a mere moment we can review all we want to accomplish in the light of love. When we get into the habit of beginning our day from the heart, all of our activities glow with the infusion of conscious intent, and all interactions occur with compassion.

We can restart our day right now by imagining how love and inspiration feel. As light glows from our heart, radiating out through our bodies into the space around us, any feelings of stress or frustration seem to melt away. Now we see each person we encounter as a fellow traveler along the journey of life, and every activity becomes part of a spiritual partnership. As conscious participants in the cycle of giving and receiving, we share our light with others as we become enlivened ourselves, with our heart leading the way.

In the intersection where the body and soul meet, our heart beats in time with the rhythm of the universe. It does the physical work of supplying our body with life force without our attention . . . but for its *spiritual* work, we need to be conscious. When we concentrate on its rhythm and glowing light, we remember that we are spiritual beings having a human experience. Then we know that we can choose any time to check in with our heart center, and in doing so, experience the joy of being in love with life.

◇ ◇ ◇

ZEN COMMUTE
DISCOVERING OURSELVES IN TRAFFIC

No one wants to be angry with a fellow human being who is lost or confused, but if we get stuck driving behind one, we may find ourselves feeling wildly, uncharacteristically impatient. It is our earnest goal to have compassion and love for other people, but when one of them cuts us off, we feel personally offended, angry, and hurt. The good news is that by experiencing these difficult emotions, we have the opportunity to see ourselves and change our approach. In that light, being stuck in traffic can become a vital part of our spiritual practice.

Sages of all faiths agree that the current moment is the only thing that really exists. The past and future are equally irrelevant in the presence of the now. Therefore, at the deepest level, there is nowhere to go, because the only place we need to be is here, now. Just reminding ourselves of this in the midst of traffic can be extraordinarily helpful. The Zen mantra "Nowhere to go / No one to be / Nothing to do" can work wonders on our panicky misperception that we need to get somewhere fast. By remaining in the moment, we inevitably get to our destination. We don't need to push or rush or panic.

Another tool used throughout the ages to maintain enlightened awareness is breath meditation. The simple act of consciously inhaling and exhaling grounds us in our bodies, reminding us where we are, who we are, and how precious our life is. When we connect deeply to our own existence in this way, many of the petty thoughts and feelings that can dominate our minds dissolve without any effort. We have breathed our way back to sanity.

From this place of awareness, you can feel compassion for the drivers who are banging their steering wheels and blaring their horns, even if they are honking at *you*. You know it is not personal; they have simply lost perspective. On your exhale, send out a wish that they, too, find the cool ease of the present moment.

◇ ◇ ◇

A GIFT OF THE HEART
LETTING PEOPLE KNOW YOU LOVE THEM

It is easy to take our feelings for granted and assume that the people we care about know how we feel about them. While they are often quite cognizant of our feelings, saying "I love you" is a gift we should give to our loved ones whenever we can. Letting others know how we feel about them is an important part of nurturing any kind of loving relationship.

Few tire of being told they are loved; and saying "I love you" can make a world of difference in someone's life, take a relationship to a new level, or reaffirm and strengthen a steady bond. Everyone needs to hear "I love you." Three simple words: *I . . . love . . . you.* When you declare your love for others, you proclaim that you care for them in the most significant way.

It can be difficult to convey your affection using words, particularly if you grew up around people who never expressed it verbally. But you should never be afraid to say "I love you" or worry that doing so will thrust you into a position of excessive vulnerability. It is important to share your feelings with those who matter to you. Part of the fulfillment that comes with loving someone is *telling* him or her that you do. Love exists to be expressed, not withheld.

If you care for someone, let the person know. Do not be afraid of the strength of your emotions or worry that your loved one will not feel the same way. "I love you" is often best said to another without expectation of a return on this investment. Since each one of us is filled with an abundance of love, there is never any concern that you will run out of it if these words are not repeated back to you.

Saying "I love you" is a gift of the heart sent directly to the heart of a recipient. Even though it may not always look that way, this is an offering that is always unconditional and given without strings attached. That is the true essence of the gift of "I love you."

◇ ◇ ◇

POWER IN NUMBERS
SENDING OUR COLLECTIVE LIGHT TO THE WORLD

Like tiny ripples that merge to form great waves, combined human intent is worth more than the sum of its parts. A single individual can initiate worldwide improvement by emitting conscious frequencies of love, beauty, goodness, and wisdom. A group of people focusing their energy on sending out light to the planet can set the stage for positive global transformation.

All of us possess the ability to channel love energy, to heal, to be a conduit for white light, and to positively influence our fellow humans from afar. Yet one person can only do so much. Imagine if each of us took a few moments at the start of every day to send out light from our hearts to the world. Mother Earth would be quickly eased, and the planet—as well as every organism and being on it—would be bathed in loving radiance. The world would be an infinitely beautiful place.

You can help bring about an earth where love triumphs over violence, air and water nourish in their purity, and people take pleasure in simply being alive. Alone, the light you emit is a wonderful healing tool, but when you join with others who share your intent to shine compassion and positive energy over the globe, a powerful force is created. Your collective consciousness and cumulative light will wash over the planet, enveloping people, communities, cities, countries, and continents.

Inviting others to do this with you can be a beautiful thing if handled delicately. People may question the benefits of sending light to an already-broken world. You will likely need to explain that each person's light joins together, and through the joining all are strengthened. Assure them that it is not the technique used, the religion practiced, or the beliefs held, but rather the *intent* that matters.

As more people come in mindfulness to send their collective light to the world, the power of their planetary gift will increase exponentially. You may already be affiliated with groups who would gladly participate in such a noble project. Children, who often feel incapable of influencing their world yet are reservoirs of innate power, are usually enthusiastic about sharing their collective light. As you gather willing people together, your individual intent will become a great and powerful wave; and you will see results in your fellow humans, in the news, and in your daily life.

◇ ◇ ◇

ACCEPTING THE GESTURE
LEARNING TO RECEIVE

As children, most of us are taught to give generously, but seldom are we provided with instructions on how to graciously *receive*. To give of ourselves — sharing our talent, our time, and our treasure — comes naturally, but being presented with a gift is often a source of embarrassment or confusion when it is not clear how to respond or we feel unworthy. Learning to receive is as much an art as giving, and it begins when we open our eyes and ears to the simple gifts that are bestowed upon us each day. If we fail to express gratitude, even for those things that seem insignificant, we are unconsciously denying the emotions of the giver. Receiving gratefully lets the individual know that he or she is valued.

Many people are uncomfortable receiving, and rather than acknowledging the spirit in which the gift was given, they disregard the sentiment with statements such as "You shouldn't have." It is easy to forget that accepting a present, a charitable service, or a compliment with grace and sincere gratitude is often a gift in itself. Expressing appreciation means letting someone experience the joy of giving.

Offerings of love, service, help, communication, or material things all possess an emotional quality and, as such, have the power to forge or strengthen bonds. In this way, accepting them necessitates yielding to another, which may cause discomfort. We are told that receiving is a form of selfishness, but when the giving is done freely and with positive intentions, our doing so actually honors both the giver and the gift.

It is necessary to care for yourself and to feel deserving before it becomes possible to accept gifts without discounting the spirit of giving or worrying about relative values. Expressing appreciation need not take long. Letting someone know that you are truly grateful for their thoughtfulness is enough. Often a simple, heartfelt "Thank you" will suffice.

Giving and receiving are both blessings, and each builds its foundation on the other. As you learn to receive, you have that much more to give. Only when you are willing to accept both openly will you truly be able to experience the magic of generosity and abundance.

◇ ◇ ◇

A TWISTING PATH
THERE ARE NO STRAIGHT LINES
IN NATURE OR IN LIFE

If you trek into the wilderness and look around with a careful gaze, you will see that the trees, flowers, and even the rocks have a tendency to flow: There is the arc of the branch that leads to the blossom, the smooth dip in a rock formation, the gnarled knot in a tree trunk, and the forking of shoots. As nature is overflowing with curves, corners, knots, and unexpected directions, so are our lives filled with unpredictable twists and turns.

While you may find yourself briefly on a straight path, there is sure to be a sudden change in route up ahead. The journey of life does not necessarily always bring you closer to your goals. In fact, sometimes you may find yourself backtracking or meandering off in a new direction. Since there is no way to foretell the outcome of your journey (just as there is no way to predict the way a new bud will form), living is in itself the path to wisdom.

Like a nature trail, this path can lead to unexpected destinations. You may be faced with direct questions such as "Who am I?" and "What is of value to me?" Or you may find yourself acquiring the answer to them through everyday experiences. The route to wisdom is only blocked when you expect it to be a straight line. It is important to remember that plans and predictions are not rigid, and as your world grows in complexity, they are likely to change. It is therefore necessary to be open to a multitude of different paths. Obstacles, weariness, curiosity, or circumstance may cause you to alter your direction abruptly. There may be forks along the way where you will need to make significant decisions based on the counsel of your inner voice.

There are both long and short roads that are sometimes curved and sometimes straight. Enjoy and learn from the adventure. Often when you look at nature, the beauty is in the unexpected. No two plants or minerals are exactly the same, and even the smallest buds curve gracefully. The winding path is often the most interesting one. The lesson you can take from that is to avoid becoming attached to what "needs" to happen and remain flexible as you continue on your journey. If you are determined to achieve certain goals, you will do so, no matter how many twists and turns you must travel.

◇ ◇ ◇

A POSITIVE SHIFT
THE ART OF FORGIVENESS

To forgive really is divine. It takes strength to set aside what is often justifiable anger. It is much easier to hold a grudge, yet when we allow ourselves to put aside that anger and forgive those who have harmed us, we actually do ourselves a great service. Making the conscious decision to let go of pain is the beginning of healing. To do so is challenging, however, because it is easy to become attached to seeing ourselves as victims and hold on to resentment, even when the person who has harmed us is genuinely sorry. Forgiving another is both one of the most difficult and one of the most spiritually rewarding choices we can make.

While forgiveness is a noble act, research shows that the person who offers it benefits as much as, and perhaps more than, those who are forgiven. Expressing true forgiveness is empowering because it helps us to stop feeling like victims and allows us to dispel our own suffering at having been wronged. Our levels of rage and hostility decrease, while our capacity to love *increases*. We are better able to control our negative emotions, and we have an enhanced ability to trust. We are freed from the control of past events, which can help us stop repeating destructive behavior. Both our physical and mental health improve. Although many people feel forgiveness is something that must be asked for or earned by another, it is actually a gift we give ourselves.

When you are ready to let go of your anger and forgive, it can be helpful to do so internally, whether or not you intend on telling the one who wronged you. It does not matter if the person has passed on or you are not in contact with one another anymore. Keep the individual you want to forgive in your mind's eye, but do not dwell on past actions or words. As you concentrate on this image, sincerely wish for the other person everything you would want for yourself. Do so as long as and as many times as it takes. It may be days, months, or even a year before you notice a change, but you will know when you are finished because you will sense a positive shift and feel free.

◇ ◇ ◇

GETTING ON TRACK
TRAINS ARE LIKE PEOPLE

The rails that crisscross the countryside and cut through cities have long captured people's imaginations. Just the idea of taking a ride on a luxury train, on an express-commuter line, or in a cargo car can evoke a sense of freedom, adventure, or romance.

Trains are like people in that they must inevitably arrive at their destinations. They make scheduled and unscheduled stops along the way and move at different speeds. Some can travel for hours and are mindful of only a single destination; others meander from busy station to busy station. The route and purpose of any train may change as the years go by. Our lives stretch out in front of us and behind us like railroad tracks; and we are the train, its passengers, and the engineer.

The way you choose to live your life and the goals you are working toward are the route and the destinations you have chosen. Like a rider on a train, you have the choice to get on and off, find new routes, pick unknown places to visit, or just stop and enjoy the view for a while. Perhaps you like to move quickly through life as if you were an express train. Or maybe you are like a commuter passenger, taking the same routes over and over. You might even want to stop just riding along and choose a different direction for your life to take.

If you have examined the tracks of your life and are feeling unsatisfied, you may want to explore the changes you can make to find a more fulfilling path to follow. Perhaps you would like to slow down a little and take a windier path rather than just traveling down the straight and narrow. Or maybe you would prefer to experience your life as more of an adventure as opposed to just a ride that gets you where you need to go. Changing your route can sometimes give you a chance to "get on the right track." You may even discover that the something new you have been waiting for is just around the bend.

◇ ◇ ◇

SEEING YOUR PERFECTION
LETTING YOUR LIGHT SHINE

We are each born into this world with unique gifts. Within us is a glimmer of the divine, a light that can potentially make the world a more beautiful place. But in many that light lies dormant, snuffed out by fears and feelings of inadequacy. To spark it is to attract attention, face the possibility of rejection or the responsibility of success, and risk being labeled immodest. Yet when we undermine it by hiding our aptitudes and quashing our dreams, we deny ourselves and others a wealth of experiences. Our abilities are a part of who we are; and when we take pride in them, we affirm the love, esteem, and trust with which we view ourselves. Moreover, as we express the light within, we grant others permission to do the same, freeing them to explore their own talents.

Some of us have been taught to hide our light from the world since childhood. Relatives caution us that the professions associated with our aptitudes are unattainable. Our peers may be envious of our skills and thus be overly critical of the activities we instinctively enjoy, and authority figures admonish us to be humble and avoid showing off. But there is a vast chasm that separates those who let their light shine and those who seek only to draw attention to themselves.

When you dare to share your light with the world, the beauty and perfection of your soul become clearly visible. You become a whole being — the literal embodiment of your vast potential. Whether you are a wonderful dancer, a first-rate cook, a whiz with numbers, or a natural negotiator, you will come to understand that you do the world no favors when you hold yourself back.

If you have hidden your light for so long that it has shrunk to an ember, make a list of everything you do well, however impractical, silly, or seemingly inconsequential. Then ask yourself how you can positively utilize those abilities in your daily life. The gifts you were born with were not granted to you arbitrarily. While you may never discover what impact your light has had on others, you can be certain that when you embrace your talents and share them, you will spread illumination in the world.

◇ ◇ ◇

SKY-BLUE HEALING
BLUE-LIGHT GUIDED MEDITATION

Please sit comfortably with your back very straight, your legs uncrossed, and your palms facing upward. If this is not comfortable for you, this meditation may be done lying down as well.

Start by imagining the color of the sky on a sunny day: sky blue.

Now, imagine that same sky-blue color to be made of light — a healing light.

Begin to breathe this in; feel it.

Imagine an opening in the top of your head. Every time you take a breath, you are inviting this color into your body, pulling it in with your breath.

Start to breathe in the blue light.

Now, begin to place it in your abdominal or pelvic area. Imagine that your pelvis is a bowl and you are going to fill it up with this beautiful blue light.

Begin to breathe it in a little harder. Passionately inhale through your nose, and push the blue light into your pelvic bowl. Make lots of noise through your nasal passages to bring in the air, and remember to exhale out your nose, not your mouth. The breath is your power.

Fill your pelvis with the blue light. Do this for a few minutes. Let your pelvis fill up with the beautiful, healing blue light.

Bring your breath back to normal now, and allow that blue light to start to rise. Permit it to move upward into your belly and your stomach. Keep letting it rise through your chest, neck, and head . . . and, finally, let it encompass your entire body.

Just be with it and feel it.

You have just done some powerful healing on yourself. Sit for a while and let it be integrated within you.

Be well.

◇ ◇ ◇

GIVING THE GIFT OF YOU
SERVING YOUR COMMUNITY

To live harmoniously, we need to be supportive and helpful to all people, creatures, and plant life that share this earth with us. While being of service is part of being a good citizen of the world, it also *feels* good to help others. When we do something for the benefit of others without the expectation of anything in return, we are turning our actions into offerings.

There are many ways to be of service to our community. There are the obvious and much-needed volunteer opportunities, such as serving a meal at a shelter, mentoring youth, or cleaning up a beach. Then there is that which we may not even think of as being an act of service.

For example, learning a new language (perhaps sign language) so that you can talk to more people is a way to reach out to others. Inviting someone who is not motivated enough to exercise on their own to join you on your daily walk is a way to give of yourself. Sharing flowers or vege-tables from your garden, organizing a poetry reading, offer-ing to babysit for a busy parent, or donating pet food to an animal shelter are all simple ways of being of service to your community.

You can also serve the world in other ways. Imagine the impact you would have on the environment if you picked up one piece of trash off the street every day and chose not to drive your car once a week. Even throwing wildflower seeds onto a vacant lot can brighten the lives of others — including those of birds and insects. Every day you can do something to make this world a better place.

During meditation, ask for guidance on what you can do to be of service. This can be a wonderful way to start your day. Smiling at a stranger who looks down in the dumps or teaching the neighborhood kids how to whistle will impact an individual's day — or even someone's life. Giving of yourself is the best gift there is.

◇ ◇ ◇

LETTING YOUR FEELINGS FLOW
TEARS

How wonderful it feels to give in and let tears flow when we are overwhelmed with emotions. Whether we are happy or sad, tears come from the soul—from our well of feelings that rises from deep down. When we give in to the prickling behind our eyes and the lump in our throat and let the drops fall from our eyes, we allow our feelings to surface so they can be set free.

Proud parents shed tears of pride over a child's accomplishments, a baby's first step, birthdays, and graduations. Long-lost friends fall into each other's arms, tears rolling down their cheeks when they reunite after years of separation.

Tears may flow from us when we are witness to a commitment being made at a wedding or even while we are watching a love story. Tears of relief may spring to our eyes when we hear that a loved one has survived an ordeal, and tears of grief may fall when we bow our head in sorrow over a loss or death. Tears born of heartache can flow as if they will never cease, whether they are for a love ended, a friendship lost, or an opportunity missed. Then, too, we shed them because of disappointment in ourselves, tragedy in the world, pain, and illness. Tears of anger can burn with emotion as they fall down our faces.

Tears offer us a physical release for our feelings. Shedding them can sometimes make us feel better, although it might seem as though they will never end once the floodgates are open. There is no shame in letting them flow freely and frequently. Tears are as natural to us as breathing is.

There is beauty in allowing yourself to be vulnerable enough to shed tears. Open up, release your tears, and let your feelings flow.

◇ ◇ ◇

A WEALTH OF FEELING
WHAT IS LOVE?

Throughout recorded history, love has burned in the hearts of composers, writers, painters, and playwrights . . . and smoldered in those of parents, children, and friends. Love—primal, passionate, and pure—has been dissected, revered, praised, and derided. It has been called complex, ethereal, and mysterious. We long for a definition but fear that the feeling called love would be less exhilarating were it defined.

Much of the mystery is rooted in the incomprehensibility of love's purpose. Self-sacrifice, procreation, caring, and romance can all exist separate from love. It is possible to have intense feelings for others but not define them as love. Yet love remains a powerful and universal force that uplifts, inspires, and is strong enough to bring about great change.

Like the wind we cannot see yet know is all around us, love is often more easily perceived through its effects. As we transcend the boundaries of ego in order to love and be loved, we put aside self-centeredness and experience unity with another. Compassion, peace, joy, excitement, and fulfillment are the inevitable results.

Paramahansa Yogananda noted that "to describe love is very difficult, for the same reason that words cannot fully describe the flavor of an orange. You have to taste the fruit to know its flavor. So with love." Those who have tasted of love often equate it with jealousy, bitterness, resentment, lust, or aggressive attachment—but it is none of those things. It is both a feeling and an action; as it brings us into the light, we strive for the happiness, safety, health, and fulfillment of those for whom we feel love.

It is true that love can be fleeting and accepts few controls or conditions. The strongest loves blaze into being and wither away in an instant . . . or last lifetimes. The one constant is the release of emotion. Love is not learned, but brought forth from within because it *is* the basic nature of humans. Only fear causes us to bury the need to love and be loved. When we accept our worthiness and reject indifference, it is then that we are able to become outlets of love.

◇ ◇ ◇

DROPPED INTO STILL WATERS
THE RIPPLE EFFECT

In a world of six billion people, it is easy to believe that the only way to initiate profound transformation is to take extreme action. Each of us, however, carries within us the capacity to change the world in small ways for better or worse. Everything we do and think affects the people in our lives, and their reactions in turn affect others. As the effect of a seemingly insignificant word passes from person to person, its impact grows and can become a source of great joy, inspiration, anxiety, or pain.

Your thoughts and actions are like stones dropped into still waters, causing ripples to spread and expand as they move outward. The impact you have on the world is greater than you could ever imagine, and the choices you make can have far-reaching consequences. You can use the ripple effect to make a positive difference and spread waves of kindness that will wash over the world.

Should the opportunity arise, the recipient of a good deed will likely feel compelled to perform one for someone else. Somebody feeling the effects of negative energy will be more likely to pass that on. One act of charity, one thoughtful deed, or even one positive thought can pass from individual to individual, snowballing until it becomes a group movement or the ray of hope that saves someone's life. Every transformation, just like every ripple, has a point of origin. You must believe in your ability to *be* that point of origin if you want to use the ripples you create to spread goodness. Consider the effect of your thoughts and actions, and try to act graciously as much as possible.

A smile directed at a stranger, a compliment given to a friend, an attitude of laughter, or a thoughtful gesture can send ripples that spread among your loved ones and associates, out into your community, and finally through the world. You have the power to touch the lives of everyone you come into contact with and everyone *those* people come into contact with. The momentum of your influence will grow as your ripples move onward and outward. One of those ripples could become a tidal wave of love and kindness.

◊ ◊ ◊

COSMIC SUPPORT
THE UNIVERSE'S PLAN FOR YOU

The path that propels us toward our dreams can be a challenging and complex one, and it is easy to get bogged down in confusion and insecurities. We often hesitate at the start of that path, questioning our purpose or our capabilities — yet we should be moving forward joyously, eager to discover what destiny has in store for us.

The universe has plans for us that eclipse anything we have dreamed of thus far. Although we must work diligently to fulfill our potential and accomplish our individual missions, the universe is aware of both the quests we chose before birth and the goals we have formulated in adulthood. If we accept that it is watching over us and believe that it will facilitate our eventual success, the universe will provide us with the assistance and opportunities that enable us to make significant progress on our journeys of ambition.

Nothing happens without a purpose. Whether we attract success or repel it depends on our willingness to stay open to a wide range of possibilities and to embrace concepts such as synchronicity. The universe is always ready to care for our needs, but we must not write off its loving attention as mere circumstance or chance. Likewise, we must endeavor to ensure that our egos do not become barriers preventing us from recognizing that even perceived mistakes and strife can be profound lessons smoothing the progress of personal evolution. When we understand that we only need to enthusiastically try our best to realize our objectives, the universe will take care of the details, propelling us forward in its unstoppable current. We may not always immediately understand the significance of certain experiences, but our trust will help us choose wisely at each crossroads.

The universe wants to see you accomplish your goals. No matter how long you have dallied or hesitated, it will always be there, ready to put its plan for you in motion at the first sign of your faith. You can make the most of this aid by acquiescing to it rather than fighting it. Nurture your dreams, but do not attempt to micromanage every detail along the way. The universe will provide you with guidance, and if you heed that wisdom, you will find that your formerly stressful quest for success will become a journey of great joy.

◇ ◇ ◇

SEEING BEYOND
THE UNKNOWN
THE FEAR OF LOSING WHAT WE HAVE

One of humanity's biggest anxieties is losing what we have. It is healthy when fear of loss helps us take steps to protect what we have worked hard to attain, but it is *un*healthy to continue to be afraid of something we can do nothing about. We need to remember that focusing our energy on fear can actually create what scares us, and holding tightly to what we have keeps us from participating in the universal flow of abundance and leads to stagnation instead. We can only really control our thoughts and our responses, so gaining proper perspective may be key to conquering such fears.

The letters of the word *fear* can be used to stand for "False Evidence Appearing Real." Fears of being separated from something or someone we feel we need for our security or happiness come from a delusion—that is, a distorted way of understanding ourselves and the world around us.

When we understand that possessions are only representations of energy at work in our lives, we are able to shift our attention to the right and proper place. We can stop fearing loss of money or success because once we know how it is created, we can always create more. We can stop fearing loss of material objects because we realize that they are not the source of our joy or well-being, but only icing on our cakes. And when we understand the energy of love, we need not hold anyone too close for fear of losing them, for we know that this emotion does not diminish when it is given or shared, but rather expands beyond boundaries of time or space.

By focusing our light on our fears, they are revealed as mere shadows that disappear in the presence of mind and spirit. We can choose instead to direct our thoughts and creative power toward things of true value — love, abundance, peace, passion, and joy. These are energies that are always available to us when we place ourselves confidently in the universal flow of abundance.

◇ ◇ ◇

EVOLVING FROM WITHIN
CHANGING YOURSELF FIRST

The world calls out for improvement, and more often than not, we are ready and willing to offer advice or admonishments. However, each of us possesses the power to effect a positive shift in energy in ourselves and in those around us. Just as purification of the soul leads to purification of the world, change within leads to change without.

Conflicts can be resolved without words. The key is changing yourself and freeing your mind. When someone or something bothers you, it helps to begin by asking yourself if you, too, possess that negative quality or are allowing yourself to be unduly affected by it. You only have control over yourself, but your influence reaches farther than you may realize. A positive change on your part often leads to positive change around you.

Your example to others is not the only way you passively inspire change. You may have altered your behavior or simply decided to adopt a shift in perspective; in doing so, you could have set into motion a series of positive consequences that bring balance.

The more we grow in virtue and the more centered we become, the more we *perceive* virtue and centeredness and the more we project them outward. As we act in ways beneficial to ourselves and others, we inspire those around us to similar action. And when we have achieved control over *our* minds and souls, we cannot be negatively affected by anything outside of ourselves. When we wish for others to change, criticism and condemnation often fail. Recognizing that none of us is perfect and that we all need to improve can be the best way to overcome conflict.

In aikido it is said: "Change yourself first before looking to change your opponent, and in the process, you might find that your opponent has changed himself." Actions, good thoughts, and positive energy speak louder than judgmental words and are the most powerful tools you can use when working toward a better world.

◇ ◇ ◇

MYSTERY OF TRANSFORMATION
THE BUTTERFLY CHRYSALIS

When a caterpillar begins life in an egg, it looks nothing like what will hatch; and the butterfly seems a far cry from the larva that precedes it. Do caterpillars recognize butterflies as their future selves? Do butterflies identify caterpillars as past relations? The most mysterious phase of this shape-shifting creature's process is that of the chrysalis: the jade-green cocoon in which the crawling, leaf-eating caterpillar transforms into a floating, nectar-drinking butterfly.

In our human lives, we sometimes find ourselves in the chrysalis state. Those times when we do not have a lot to offer the outside world, it is because, whether we realize it or not, much of our energy is consumed with an inner transition. We might feel sluggish or uninterested in what surrounds us. We might feel impatient with ourselves, wondering why we do not have the energy we used to for our usual routines. But if we remember the chrysalis — the dark inner sanctum that provides the environment for a remarkable conversion — we can relax and let ourselves be, finding ways to support our process rather than coaxing ourselves away from it.

If you see a butterfly emerging from its chrysalis, the temptation may be to help it break out. The physical challenge of this part of the process is necessary, though, for the butterfly to build its strength so that it can survive outside. The same is true of us: Sometimes we have to labor on our own to discover the force we need to be our new selves in the world. Similarly, when seeing friends or family members struggling, it is easy to become impatient and want to help with their emergence, but we have to learn to let others make their own way.

Taking on the challenge of liberating ourselves enables us to thrive in our new freedom. Sometimes the greatest support we can offer others and ourselves is patience and quiet confidence in the process unfolding, along with faith that the result will be extraordinary.

◇ ◇ ◇

WISDOM OF THE SAGES
HONORING OUR ELDERS

There is a reason why wisdom is associated with age. Traditionally, elders have been the wise men and women of communities. Most spiritual leaders apprenticed for the majority of their lives before beginning their practice. In many parts of the world, elders are honored and respected for the wisdom they have gained through life experience. They are considered to be a valuable source of knowledge and have an important role to fulfill in passing on traditions and customs.

In many corners of the globe, nursing homes for the elderly are rare. Caring for one's aging parents is considered an honor and a blessing. In other cultures it is not uncommon for three or four generations to live together under one roof. Immediate families consist of children, parents, grandparents, great-grandparents, and sometimes great-aunts and great-uncles. Such intergenerational coexistence is beneficial to all. There are caregivers for both young children and the elderly, and older relatives can pass down the family history to, and act as role models for, younger family members.

In Native American culture, elders are appreciated for their close connection to nature and the spiritual world. They are known as "wisdomkeepers," acting as caretakers of the planet. Respected for their life experience and wisdom, African elders serve as mediators between deceased ancestors and living family members.

Honoring and respecting our elders is a way of building community and strengthening society. It helps us appreciate every stage of life and view aging in a positive light. After all, hopefully we ourselves will have the opportunity to become sages in our later years.

◇ ◇ ◇

WORKING CONNECTION
EVERY JOB IS IMPORTANT

As children, we dreamed big dreams. We wanted to be — or were told by our parents that we *should* be — doctors, lawyers, or scientists. As time passed and we grew, our paths naturally evolved. Those jobs still held their appeal, but we understood a subtle truth: The world needs us to fill our own role. Perhaps we also discovered that we were better suited to other work, or we wanted immediate employment. Often, though, the old idea of a "good" occupation has remained fixed, and it is easy to overlook the fact that all jobs are important to the economy and to the souls of the people who hold them.

You do not have to be in the healing-arts industry or work for a charity or nonprofit organization to feel good about what you do. Everything is connected, everything flows, everybody is important — from the janitor to the secretary to the CEO. Without one there cannot be the other.

If you are unhappy in your job, take a moment to stop and think about how what you do is connected to other people. See the oneness. Does your smile and radiant energy help others through their day? If your job is to file all day long, be the best filing person there ever was. Take pride in your work, for without it, how would anybody find what they need to do *their* job?

There is importance in every job that cannot be measured in numbers or in prestige and can only be found within the heart of the man or woman doing it. The happiest people — those who believe they have the best jobs — are the ones who respect the work they do no matter what it is. When we understand that, it becomes obvious that every job is worthy of praise.

◇ ◇ ◇

LISTING MAGNIFICENCE
FIVE THINGS I LIKE ABOUT MYSELF

Our primary relationship in life is with ourselves. No one else goes through every experience in life with us. We are our one permanent companion . . . yet we are often our own worst critic. To remind ourselves of our magnificence, we can do the following exercise: "Five Things I Like about Myself."

Begin by writing down at least five things that you like about yourself. This is not the time to be modest. If you are having trouble coming up with a total of five items, you know that this exercise can really benefit you. Be sure to include more than physical attributes on your list, since your body is only part of who you are. If you are still struggling, think of what you like about your favorite people, because these traits are probably qualities that you possess, too. Another way to complete your list is to call to mind five things you do *not* like about yourself and find something about these traits that you *can* like.

Continue this process for a week, thinking of five new things you like about yourself every day. At the end of the week, read the list aloud to yourself while standing in front of a mirror. Instead of looking for flaws to fix, allow the mirror to reflect your magnificence. You may feel silly standing before a mirror and reading aloud a list of your admirable attributes, but it might just bring a smile to your face and change the way you see yourself. Remember that when you feel the most resistant, this exercise can benefit you the most.

Since we are constantly looking at the world instead of at ourselves, we do not often see what is magnificent about us in the way that others do. When we take the time to experience ourselves as we would someone we love and admire, we become our best companion and supporter on life's journey.

◇ ◇ ◇

PLUNGING INTO THE DEEP
LIFE CAN BE SCARY

Life can take us on a roller-coaster ride full of highs and lows and twists and turns. It is frightening to suddenly find ourselves heading for a deep plunge — even for those of us who enjoy unexpected thrills — yet this feeling happens to all of us. At these moments, it is important to remember that we are not alone in our experiences. No matter how brave, strong, or levelheaded we are, sometimes we all get scared.

Our fears may revolve around our physical safety, particularly if we are not feeling well, are living under difficult circumstances, or are doing work that exposes us to hazardous conditions. Or we may be experiencing financial woes that are causing us to be anxious about making ends meet. We might also fear the loss of a loved one who is sick or be scared of never finding someone special to spend our life with. We could be frightened to start at a new school, begin a different job, move to a new town, or meet new people. Whatever our fears are, they are valid, and we do not need to feel ashamed or embarrassed that we are, at times, afraid.

It may be comforting to know that everyone gets scared — and that is perfectly okay. Sometimes just acknowledging our fears is enough to make us feel better. And while it occasionally takes a lot more to ease our minds, we can console ourselves with the knowledge that life *can* be scary at times. Giving ourselves permission to be afraid lets us move through our fears so we can release them. It also makes it all right to relay them to others. Sharing our apprehensions with other people can make them less overwhelming, because we are not letting them grow inside of us as pent-up emotions. Sharing our fears can also lighten our burden, since we are not carrying our worries all by ourselves.

Remember that you are not alone.

◇ ◇ ◇

GIVING OF HERSELF
MOTHER

Mothers throughout history have been worshipped, revered, analyzed, and even criticized. Every one of us was created through the wondrous workings of a woman's body; each of us has a mother.

But being a mother is more than a biological concept. In India, women who are profoundly nurturing, compassionate, and wise are publicly acknowledged with the title "Holy Mother." Those who have never met their birth mothers often feel that they have this figure in adoptive parents, relations, and friends. There are human and spiritual mothers, Mother Earth, and mother goddesses. The maternal role is infinitely complex and is one of pure tenderness, compassion, and unflagging loyalty. The mother represents fertility, stability, creation, and sacrifice.

Our mothers determine who we become because they are not only life givers, but are the most influential people in our young lives. Before we are old enough to understand that influence, mothers bestow upon us the beginnings of our spirituality and value systems. A mother lauds accomplishment and ignores minor faults. She teaches her children, shields them from misfortune, and hides her own tears, preferring to laugh so that her sons and daughters can laugh with her. She is both a sharer of grief and a healer of many pains. And every mother gives of herself knowing that someday her progeny will leave her.

For these reasons and more, motherhood is a sacred institution not limited by narrow constraints. It is also not unusual to seek maternal guidance in a wise female or a grandmother, because each woman is taught to *be* a mother by her own, whether she has children or not. Other ways to see a mother is to find a source of motherly nurturing in the planet, which gives us so much and demands little in return. The earth mother continually blesses us with her bounty, and we are born and eventually go back to the universal mother.

The definition is necessarily broad, because mothers of all types exist—in part to put a smooth veneer on the rough edges of life for those they love. A mother never ceases growing, never stops becoming more motherly. Although some may argue that she is a woman who gives life with her womb and nourishment with her breast, it is important to remember that a mother—any mother—is also one who gives life with her *tenderness* and nourishment with her *love*.

◇ ◇ ◇

TRANSFORMING NEGATIVE INTO POSITIVE
TONGLEN MEDITATION

Just as pain can grow exponentially, so can compassion and love be inspired in countless others. All it takes is a single individual who chooses to transform negative energy into goodness. One method of doing this is the Buddhist practice of *tonglen meditation,* wherein you consciously draw suffering into yourself and release positive energy with each focused breath. In *The Tibetan Book of Living and Dying,* this meditation is described as breathing in what is to be healed and transforming it through the power of your own heart and that of Buddha. Then, in breathing out, you project what was transformed in your heart into those of others.

Earnest tonglen meditation begins when you release yourself from the misconception that pushing negative things away while drawing good ones to yourself is of utmost importance. This may entail ten or more minutes of meditation to clear the mind of distractions, or simply preparing it by entering your stillest mental space and imagining your heart becoming free and full of love. Then, inhale with the awareness that you are bringing energy into yourself. Access your reference points for pain and for joy, acknowledge both, and recognize that you have the power to transform one into the other. Exhale with the awareness that you are projecting positive, loving energy not only throughout your immediate environment, but also the world.

Your first reaction to this practice may be that it is counterintuitive. This is a natural response. But tonglen revolves around balance, around giving and receiving. You cannot get lost in the negative aspects of the world, for in breathing out, you are a beacon of joy. Similarly, you cannot turn a blind eye to sorrow because you bear its weight.

Tonglen meditation can be practiced on a personal scale or a universal one, depending on where you perceive immediate need. It is as simple as breathing—and yet, in practicing tonglen, you give the greatest gift you can: that of healing.

◇ ◇ ◇

PERSONAL TALES
WRITING YOUR STORY

Everyone at one time or another has wanted to express his or her story. Writing a memoir to read privately, share with family or friends, or publish is an emotionally satisfying way to gain perspective on your experiences while sharing your unique voice. We have all experienced feelings and events in our lives that we long to write down. Giving in to that urge can provide you with an outlet for purging any frustration, anxiety, or long-dormant feelings.

No one else has to read your story. You may even want to write it without reading it right away. Satisfying the need to tell your story is not predicated upon your writing ability. It does, however, take effort to set down the truth in detail. Your memories—captured on paper as descriptive scenes, sights, sounds, and scents—may at first seem disconnected or incomplete. Rest assured that you possess the ability to shape your recollections into stories.

Everyone wants to be heard, and reading your story to others can meet that need. Writing it can also help you understand your life experiences . . . and when you finish, you may be surprised by what you have accomplished. Your story can encompass as much or as little of your life as you prefer. You may surprise yourself with new insights; or you may find yourself exploring your roots, your identity, and your future through your words. Allow your writing to guide you, and be as truthful as possible. Do not worry about what others will think of your personal journey, your style of writing, or your words.

Penning a personal narrative filled with feelings and perceptions can create long-term health benefits. As you write, remember to have compassion for yourself, particularly when describing traumatic events. If you are a young person, you can add to your life story as you grow older. Your writing may help family members know you better, or they may understand themselves more through reading about your experiences. Most important, you are expressing yourself in a permanent way, giving a gift to yourself, and letting your voice be heard.

◇ ◇ ◇

GREEN ENERGY
THE SPIRITUAL ENERGY OF MONEY

Most of us are intimately connected to money. Whether we are spending it or making it, money is a part of our lives. It makes sense, then, for us to cultivate a healthy relationship with it. Like so many other things in life, that begins with having a good attitude.

How you perceive money has a great deal to do with how much you have and are able to create. While it is not healthy to be preoccupied with it or lust after it, it is important to appreciate its value and the positive things it can do for your life. And the more you appreciate something, the more you invite that into your flow. If you express thankfulness and gratitude for love, health, and money, you will attract more of those things into your life. Likewise, if you have a negative attitude toward such things, you will draw less of them into your life. So if you are constantly worrying about a lack of money, you will consistently have financial woes, even if you earn a good income.

51

Be conscious of your thoughts toward money. Do you feel as if you deserve to have it? How were you raised to deal with it? Were you always urged to save and never spend, or were you constantly told there was never enough?

There is energy in everything, and money is no exception. The energy of earning manifests itself in money and is exchanged through spending. Therefore, it is important that we not only make money, but that we spend it as well. Anything that is static will never reproduce, and that includes money. Still, you should use it not only to take care of your needs, but to help others as well. Be as generous as you can with those less fortunate and you will be circulating your money so that more comes back to you.

◇ ◇ ◇

OBSERVING EVOLUTION
ALLOWING OTHERS TO WALK THEIR PATHS

Watching loved ones or peers traverse a path littered with stumbling blocks can be immensely painful. We instinctively want to guide them toward a safer track and share with them the wisdom we have acquired through experience. All human beings have the right to carve out their own paths, however, without being unduly influenced by outside interference. To deny them that right is to deny them enlightenment, since true insight cannot be conveyed in lectures.

Each individual must earn independence and illumination by making decisions and reflecting upon the consequences of every choice. In allowing others to walk their paths freely, you honor their right to express their humanity in whatever way they see fit. Although you may not agree or identify with their choices, understand that all people must learn in their own way and at their own pace.

The events and circumstances that shape our lives are unique because each of us is unique. What touches one person deeply may do nothing more than irritate or confound another. Therefore, we are all drawn to different paths — the ones that will have the most profound effects on our personal evolution.

If you feel compelled to intervene when watching other human beings plodding slowly and painfully down a difficult path, try to empathize with their need to grow autonomous and make their own way in the world. Should these people ask for your aid, give it freely. You can even tell them about *your* path or offer advice in a conscious, loving way. Otherwise, give them the space they need to make mistakes, enjoy the fruits of their labors, revel in their triumphs, and discover their own truths.

The temptation to direct the course of others is a creature of many origins. Overactive egos can convince us that ours is the one true path or awaken a craving for control within us. But each person is entitled to seek out his or her own road leading from the darkness into the light. When we celebrate those paths and encourage the people navigating them, we not only enjoy the privilege of watching others grow, we also reinforce our dedication to diversity, independence, and individuality.

◇ ◇ ◇

UNDERSTANDING ONENESS
LEVELS OF CONSCIOUSNESS

Sometimes we look at the actions of others and find it difficult to understand what motivates them. But we are all doing the best we can with the information we currently have. We have all been taught how to see the world from the examples of those around us and by our experiences. Keeping this in mind, we can accept the choices made by others while seeking ways to increase the world's level of consciousness as a whole.

Our different levels of consciousness are like the developmental stages of children, whose understanding varies according to age and experience. For example, the behavior of a 2-year-old who does not want to share can be understood as a phase of his or her social education, whereas a 16-year-old who behaves in the same manner would be viewed as acting childish. It is important to remember that we are each on our own unique path. We may have chosen certain lessons or made an agreement to play particular roles in the unfolding of the world's understanding before we incarnated in this lifetime, so our job is not to judge others, but to shift the balance of understanding on the earth by increasing our own.

Every thought we have and action we take becomes part of the collective energy of the planet. When we use our energy to bring light into the world, it combines with that of others to dispel the darkness. Although we live in a world of duality, which helps acquaint us with the material plane, we do not need to experience extremes in order to understand them. We can share our experiences and understanding with others not from a place of condescension, but of connection. When the entire family of humanity recognizes that each of our thoughts, choices, and actions affects us all, we will share an incredible level of consciousness — one that puts our oneness above all else and helps us evolve into higher expressions of our spiritual selves.

The next time you witness an incomprehensible action by another, remember that this person is of the same earth as you but simply on a different conscious level at this point in life. Find compassion, bless the person, and move along through your day in grace.

◇ ◇ ◇

EMBRACING UNPREDICTABILITY
WHEN LIFE THROWS YOU A CURVEBALL

In life we are always setting goals for ourselves and working to make them happen. This gives us focus and ensures that we use our time and energy efficiently and effectively. It also provides us with a sense of purpose and direction. We know where we are headed and what we want to do, although quite often, due to forces outside our control, things do not go as we had planned — the flat tire on the way to the wedding, for instance, or the unforeseen flu virus — and we have to adjust to a postponement or create a whole new set of circumstances. Even positive turns of fortune — an unexpected influx of cash or falling in love — require us to be flexible and to reconsider our plans and priorities, sometimes in the blink of an eye. This is what happens when life throws us a curveball.

The ability to accept what is happening and let go of our original expectations is key when dealing with these unexpected turns of fate. We have a tendency to get stuck in our heads, clinging to an idea of how we think life should go, and we can have a hard time accepting anything that does not comply with that idea.

The fact is that life is unpredictable. The trip you thought was for business—and got depressed about when the deal fell through—actually landed you at the airport two days earlier than planned so you could meet the love of your life. Your car breaks down and you are late for an appointment. While it is true that you never arrive at that important meeting, you end up spending a few relaxing hours with people you would never have met otherwise.

Remember that not only are curveballs the universe's way of keeping us awake—which is a gift in and of itself— but they are also its method of bringing us wonderful surprises. Next time one comes your way, take a deep breath, say thank you, and open your mind to a new opportunity.

◇ ◇ ◇

PATIENT PERSEVERANCE
DRAWING STRENGTH FROM PLANTS

Each season, grasses, flowers, shrubs, and trees let a part of themselves go in the form of seeds, every one of which is a point of life containing the full potential of the parent. In the quest to find a rooting spot, they are buffeted by winds, parched by the sun, and soaked by rain. And, as likely as not, they encounter cement or stone rather than fertile soil.

Each season the seeds find what space they can and put forth their roots, slowly creating more room for themselves and pushing ever upward, even when the new world they discover is harsh and unpredictable. Seedlings are small, but a single plant can widen a crack in a sidewalk or turn a rock to dust through nothing more than patient perseverance.

In our lives, it is not uncommon to find ourselves cast into the wind, through our own choices or through fate. We are blown hither and thither by fear, uncertainty, and the influence of others. The obstacles we face may seem insurmountable and the challenges too much to bear.

When this happens, look around you and note the seemingly desolate and inhospitable places in which plants have thrived. Given little choice, they set down their roots and hold on tightly, making the best of their situation. Then examine your own circumstances. Ask yourself if there is an unimagined source of strength that you can tap into. Look to the future—picture a time in which you have widened a place for yourself and have flourished through your difficulties.

The smallest things in life—such as these tiny sprouts—given time and the will to forge on, can overcome any circumstance and break down huge barriers. It may be tempting, however, when you are faced with rough or uncertain odds, to give up, change direction, or choose the easiest path. Despite this, within you there exists the same resolve and fortitude as that displayed by these courageous plants. In finding yourself in a tight spot, you, too, can look upward, grab hold where you can, and use your determination to reach new heights.

◇ ◇ ◇

COMING OUT OF HIDING
ISOLATION

There are times in our lives when withdrawing from our social obligations and taking some time to be alone is necessary to rejuvenate our energy and renew our connection to ourselves. However, there are also occasions when withdrawal is a red flag, indicating an underlying sense of depression or some other problem. We may not even have consciously decided to isolate ourselves but wake up one day to find that we have been spending most of our time alone. Perhaps friends who used to call have given up. With no one inviting us out, we sink deeper into alienation.

The longer our isolation lasts, the harder it is to reach out to people. It is as if we have failed to exercise a particular muscle, and now it is so weak that we do not know how to use it. In order to return to a healthy, balanced state of being, however, reaching out is exactly what we need to do.

If you find yourself in this situation, call an understanding friend who will listen to you with compassion, not a defensive one who may have taken your withdrawal personally. The last thing you need is to be chided; a negative response could intensify your isolation. If you do not have a kind friend you can rely on, call a spiritual counselor or therapist who may be able to assist you in determining the underlying cause of your isolation and help you find your way out of it.

When you have been in a pattern of secluding yourself, reentering the world of friendships, conversations, and group activities can begin to seem impossible . . . but with time you will. If you make the effort to explain that you have fallen out of touch and would like to reconnect, most people will understand. Take your time and be gentle with yourself, starting with one person and building from there. Try to reach out to a different individual every week. Before you know it, you will find yourself back in the company of friends.

◇ ◇ ◇

CONSCIOUS COOKING
PREPARING FOOD WITH INTENTION

We are what we eat, but more important, we *affect* what we eat — from the cutting board to the pot to the table. The health-imparting properties of food, also known as the life force, are subtly changed by the way in which we prepare it and the spiritual qualities we project into it.

Thoughts and emotions, both positive and negative, are absorbed by food as it is prepared. Think of the powerful healing properties of what you have cooked for a sick relative or friend. Chicken soup is simply that until it is prepared with the intent to heal. As you cook, your intentions — be they loving, sad, destructive, creative, or joyful — are infused into the food. And food prepared with positive intent provides nourishment not only for the body, but also for the soul.

Before you can begin cooking consciously or with intent, it is necessary to remove sources of unpleasantness or distraction. Transform your kitchen into a comfortable, relaxing, and nurturing space. Concentrate on positive thoughts each time you enter it, because negativity can affect the taste and nutritional value of the meals you make. It may be helpful to think of food preparation as a type of meditation in which your thoughts are free of the "buzz" of the world and are centered and focused on the task at hand: cutting vegetables, measuring liquids, blending spices, and adding herbs.

Devote the same amount of time and energy to simple tasks as you would to the preparation of a complex recipe, as this honors the processes involved in cooking. As you work, concentrate on nourishment and feelings of love. If you like, you may want to speak, chant, or sing a blessing over the ingredients before they are prepared to impart your positive intent. Finally, be present in the cooking process from beginning to end by paying attention to the beauty of your ingredients and the magical way in which they blend to become something new.

A Zen saying instructs cooks to "see the pot as your own head, and see the water as your life's blood." Consciously and lovingly cleansing, peeling, chopping, and stirring ingredients bring you closer to your food and, in consequence, to those to whom you serve it. During preparation—as your soul exists in the moment to give nourishment—your meals will be a source of intense life-force energy and joy to you and others.

◇ ◇ ◇

REGARDLESS OF OUTCOME
THERE ARE NO "WRONG" DECISIONS

Many of us have a hard time making decisions. We fear that if we choose the wrong partner, then we will be stuck in an unhappy relationship, or if our financial choice is the incorrect one, we will make a bad investment. Yet there are no wrong decisions. Perhaps we could, at times, make different ones with respect to our relationships, personal pursuits, careers, or the right color of paint to buy for our bedroom. Regardless of the outcome, though, we always gain valuable experience or insights from any choice we make.

Making any decision is always better than making none at all. At least we had the courage to decide, take a chance, and make a move in a particular direction. We cannot take action unless we come to a decision first. And it is never wrong, because we always gain something from it — whether we get what we intended or learn a valuable lesson. Sometimes we need to follow through on a decision to realize that we do not really want what we thought we did.

For instance, maybe you always wanted to live in a big city, so you leave family, friends, and a secure job in a small town to move across the country. However, once you get there, you find out that you do not really like urban life. You never would have known that unless you tried it, so you move back home, all the more appreciative of small-town living. Rather than constantly wondering what else is out there, you are now able to fully embrace your surroundings and the direction your life there is taking. Your decision to move to the city *did* work out—just not in the way you had envisioned.

While your decisions may not always lead you to what you thought you wanted, you always end up with what will ultimately make you happiest. Being able to make choices is one of life's privileges. Exercise your right to fearlessly decide.

◇ ◇ ◇

FINDING THE GIFT
BAD DAYS

We all have days when it feels as if the world is against us or that the chaos we are experiencing will never end. One negative circumstance seems to lead to another. We may wonder on such a day whether anything in our life will ever go right again.

But a bad day, like any other, can be a gift, showing you that it is time to slow down, change course, or lighten up. It could help you glean wisdom you might otherwise have overlooked or discounted. Bad days can certainly cause you to experience uncomfortable feelings you would prefer to avoid, yet they may also give you a potent means of learning about yourself.

You may consider a bad day to be one where you have missed an important meeting because your car stalled, the dryer broke, or you received a piece of very disheartening news earlier in the morning. Multiple misfortunes that take place one after the other can leave you feeling vulnerable and intensely cognizant of your fragility, although bad days can only have a long-term negative effect on you if you let them. It is better to ask yourself what you can learn from these kinds of days. They may be an indicator that you need to stay in and hibernate or let go of your growing negativity.

Bad days contribute to the people we become. Although we may feel discouraged and distressed, they can teach us patience and perseverance. It is important to remember that our attitude drives our destiny and that one negative experience does not have to be the beginning of an ongoing stroke of bad luck. A bad day is memorable because it is situated among many good ones; otherwise, we would not even bother to acknowledge it as bad.

Know, too, that everybody has bad days. You are not alone — the world is not against you. Tomorrow is a brand-new day . . . greet it with love and watch it unfold into, perhaps, a better one.

◇ ◇ ◇

GIVING THE FREEDOM TO LIVE
ACCEPTING THE JOURNEYS OF OTHERS

In life each of us walks on the special path that the soul is destined to undertake. Our journeys are very different, and we progress at different rates. The pitfalls and blessings we encounter are unique, yet we are all learning, and no one form of knowledge is more important than any other.

Even so, when we observe those around us, it can be easy to pass judgment on their decisions and assume that their actions will correspond with what we feel is right. But for every problem, there are a multitude of solutions. Everyone makes their own choices, and it is important that we accept each person's unique way of doing things, even if watching can be frustrating. Giving others the freedom to act in the way they feel is best without the fear of harsh judgments honors the capacity for growth that all people possess.

It is helpful to practice accepting others as they are. Never judge their decisions based on the path you would have taken, because every person lives by different values and experiences. Challenge is a universal concept, but we all deal with difficulties in our own way.

Give others the space to choose as they will, but do not harden your heart against their experience. It is not wise to try to fix people or control situations. You may feel compelled to intervene when difficulties arise, but it is important only to offer guidance when asked, unless people are involved in a truly dangerous situation or cannot act for themselves. To not choose the perceived right path or make enlightened decisions is simply another step on the journey—one that is a means of gaining experience and wisdom. Letting go of the need to influence others does not preclude offering them loving support, and it does not imply that you need to stop caring. It *does* mean stepping back, dissolving judgment, and gracefully allowing them to live out their own destinies.

Giving others the liberty to blossom in *their* journeys grants you the freedom to take more notice of your own. You may not condone the actions you see taking place, but by letting them be, your reactions will be more loving, and you will be able to focus on just being yourself, confident that the path you take is as right, valid, and special as any other.

◇ ◇ ◇

LIGHTENING THE SOUL
SOUL EVOLUTION

From the moment we are born, our souls may feel heavy because they are carrying the weight of all we have lived, loved, and learned in our past incarnations. It is only when we actively seek to work through our issues that we can lighten the load and our souls can evolve. Divesting ourselves of what no longer serves us—such as unwarranted fear, the inability to feel empathy, or self-limiting behaviors—is just one of the many challenges we may encounter in this lifetime. While some issues we face are easier to deal with since they are the final remains of residue from a past life, others offer greater challenges because we are meant to work through them during *this* lifetime.

Often we expect ourselves to recover quickly from difficult or painful circumstances. When we do not or *can*not, we may feel emotionally inept or hopeless. The evolution of the soul, however, is an ongoing process that can take many lifetimes. It is a matter of accepting that even when we do our best, there are going to be situations, people, and outcomes that we cannot control. It is also important to remember that our experiences now may be setting the groundwork for future healing, whether in this life or the next. The more we release each time, the more we grow and the more our souls will evolve.

Although it is not always possible to work through all of your issues in a single lifetime, it is essential that you confront what you are called to face in this one and learn what you need to. It is also important to remember that the most effective way to let your soul grow is to be an active participant in life. Be present in each moment and your soul will do this work for you.

◇ ◇ ◇

BEING WHO YOU ARE
LIVING YOUR TRUTH

When we are young children, we live authentically, seldom afraid or embarrassed to seek out what we want or to speak our minds. As we grow older, we tend to tuck that authenticity away, putting it aside while we chase our dreams, afraid that it might hinder us in our success . . . but we never let that freedom go completely. We may conform publicly to society's expectations while embracing secret passions when alone. We may withhold certain opinions, although this does not change the fact that we possess them.

It is important, however, never to stray too far from that youthful brashness and self-interest, for they are qualities that help make you who you are. The authentic you is your true self; and in living authentically, you make time for the things you love and project who you really are. The simplest way to live your truth is to leave the expectations of others behind and act in the way you feel is most worthwhile.

To do so, it takes being selfish in a healthy way by doing what you know is best for you, regardless of the opinions of others — even those of close friends and family. Living authentically means that you make choices without fear, trusting in your soul's wisdom. If you value personal pursuits, do not feel forced into a certain job just to make enough money to keep up with your neighbors. Conversely, if you prize success in business, do not let others' perception of what is right for you hold you back. Denying your unique truth can lead to feelings of failure and dissatisfaction because you are not acknowledging your authentic self. In living your truth, there are no pretenses. Everything you do will reflect who you truly are.

If you are unsure of who the authentic you really is, look inward and ask yourself what your purpose, values, and needs are. Honor your strengths, and try not to let yourself be guided by what others expect of you. Finally, discover your passions by trying new things and sticking with those that stir your soul. Finding who you really are and then making the choice to embrace your true dreams and desires will take your life in a direction that is both satisfying and deeply meaningful.

◇ ◇ ◇

HONORING TRANSITION
THE BEAUTY OF DEATH

Death is as much a part of life as birth. Most of us are thrilled to witness a newborn's arrival into this world, but it is also an honor to be with loved ones when they pass on. While there is always sadness in losing someone, if we open our minds to the beauty of death, we can understand that it is as powerful a transition as birth.

Most people do not want to be alone when they die. By being at the bedside of our loved ones when they are dying, we can help them have a more peaceful, sacred end to physical life. Often those dying have unfinished business, such as making peace with others, healing old wounds, and forming a spiritual connection if they do not already have one. People near death are often more honest and real than at any other time in their lives except, perhaps, for infancy. Being able to stay with someone during that period allows for incredible bonding.

We can help loved ones prepare for their final journey by making them as comfortable as possible. If we are fortunate enough to be able to have them at home, we want to make sure, if at all possible, that they are not in pain and have the proper medical attention they need. After that, we can provide them with such comforts as flowers, music, and a favorite blanket or clothing item. Even if they are hospitalized, we can sit and talk with them, read to them, massage them, rub their feet, or just hold their hands.

To help them on their spiritual journey, talk about rituals they might find comforting; bring treasured objects that they can reflect on; recite poems or spiritual verses together; light candles or incense, if possible; sing and/or play music; or simply sit with them in silence.

Allow yourself to feel blessed to be at someone's deathbed. Know that your being there can bring a sense of peace, reconciliation, and acceptance of this passage to both you and the other person. In accepting death, hopefully you will no longer fear it and be able to see the actual beauty in it.

◇ ◇ ◇

FIXING A BAD DAY
RESCUE TOOLBOX FOR COPING

When times are tough and you are experiencing stress, it is nice to have some tools that you can call upon to help get through a rough patch and use on an ongoing basis to make your life a little easier. It is best to remember that you are not alone, even though sometimes you feel as if nobody understands you.

The following is a Rescue Toolbox for Coping. When you are at the end of your rope, open your toolbox, take a breath, and care for yourself.

— **Call a friend.** Talk about it. Calling a friend who will listen willingly and openly can make all the difference. Sometimes we feel as though we do not want to "dump" on people, but wouldn't you want your friends to call you when *they* need someone?

— **Write about it.** Journal. Get your thoughts out of your head and onto paper.

— **Take a bath.** Make yourself a bath with sea salt to release and renew. It will help cleanse your energy field, which is just as important as getting the clutter out of your head. While you are in your bath, imagine all bad thoughts and negative energy going down the drain to Mother Earth.

— **Walk around the block.** Physical exercise is very important in helping relieve stress, but many of us do not have a regular routine at the gym or yoga studio.

— **Meditate . . .** whatever this means to you. Meditation does not always have to be sitting in a lotus position or chanting. Sometimes the act of folding the laundry can be a meditation, as can gardening, knitting, or cooking. It is important to relieve your mind of daily complications and give yourself quiet time to be still.

— **Commune with nature.** Getting out into nature in some way is very rejuvenating. This can take any form you like, including gardening, walking in the park, riding a horse, watching a sunset, swimming in a lake, or taking a leisurely stroll through a field. Enjoy nature on a regular basis — it is very grounding, and your soul will sing.

— **Thank your body.** Thank every cell, organ, muscle, and bone in your body for doing such a great job in supporting you. Imagine how your physical self feels every time you make a negative comment or put it down. Thank your body and see what an amazing difference it makes in your day — and in your life.

◇ ◇ ◇

PEELING AWAY THE LAYERS
TREES SHEDDING THEIR BARK

Trees grow up through their branches, and down through their roots into the earth. They also grow wider with each passing year. As they do, they shed the bark that served to protect them but is no longer big enough to contain them. In the same way, we create boundaries and develop defenses to shield ourselves, and at a certain point we outgrow them. If we do not allow ourselves to shed our protective layer, we cannot expand into our full potential.

Trees need their protective bark to enable the delicate process of growth and renewal to unfold without threat. Likewise, we must have our boundaries and defenses so that the more vulnerable parts of ourselves can safely heal and unfold. But our growth also depends upon our ability to soften, loosen, and discard boundaries and defenses that we no longer need. It is often the case in life that structures we put in place to help us grow eventually become constricting.

Unlike a tree, we must *consciously* decide when it is time to shed our bark and expand our boundaries so that we can move into our next ring of growth. Many spiritual teachers have suggested that our egos do not disappear so much as they become large enough to hold more than just our small sense of self; the boundary of self widens to contain people and beings other than just "me." Each time we shed a layer of defensiveness or ease up on a boundary that we no longer need, we metaphorically become bigger people.

With this in mind, it is important that we take time to question our boundaries and defenses. While it is essential to uphold and honor the protective barriers we have put in place, it is equally critical that we soften and release them when the time comes. In doing so, we create the space for our next phase of growth.

◇ ◇ ◇

CONSCIOUS INSPIRATION
BEING CREATIVE EVERY DAY

Many people harbor the idea that there are two kinds of people in the world: creative and noncreative. You often hear certain individuals saying, "I wish I were creative."

Actually, we are all inherently creative. As human beings, creativity is our birthright. We use it to get through each and every day in simple tasks such as picking out what to wear or choosing the words we use to express ourselves. Not only is it natural for us to be creative, it is also healthy. Experts say that conscious creativity is as good for our overall sense of well-being as exercising, eating right, and getting enough sleep.

When we are "in the zone" with our creativity, we move into a different experience of time and space; hours pass like minutes, and we sometimes literally forget where we are. Our logical mind, which generally runs the show, takes a backseat to imagination and intuition, creating a feeling of spaciousness, calm, and release. When we return to the grid of everyday reality, we see with new eyes.

You can easily access your creativity throughout the day with simple exercises. At work, take a moment to re-arrange the items on your desk or wall, maybe replacing old photographs or objects with new images that inspire new thoughts. Just five minutes devoted to this simple creative act can noticeably refresh your mind. To elevate your entire day into a more creative zone, take your camera with you and document one full day in your life.

The benefits of creativity are in the doing. The finished product, while wonderful, is almost beside the point. What matters most is the experience of being awake and relaxed in the flow of our lives.

◇ ◇ ◇

UNEXPECTED FEAR
PANIC ATTACKS

The symptoms of panic attacks can vary from person to person, and chances are, you know somebody who has them — or maybe that somebody is *you*. Symptoms can be a feeling of impending doom or terror, loss of control, and heart-attack-like sensations.

Many of these symptoms come from the instinctive "fight or flight" response that arises when the mind perceives a dangerous situation. These episodes may come unexpectedly or in predictable circumstances such as driving, being in crowds, or riding in an elevator. Many people hide the fact that they suffer from panic attacks; but it is important to remember that they are common, survivable, and treatable.

When one comes on, accept that it is happening but know that it will pass, and ease yourself through it while remaining as relaxed as possible. If necessary, try to focus on the fact that nothing bad is going to happen to you and that you are not crazy or about to die.

If you suffer from panic attacks, here are some tools that can help you—as an example, this is a situation involving driving:

1. Before you get into your car, take time to write about what you are scared of. It is important to reach the root of what is causing your attacks.

2. If you have a cell phone, attach it to a headset and dial a friend. Tell the other person that there is no need to speak; you merely want a friend on the line while you are driving, just to know that someone else is there.

3. If you start to panic, take a moment to realize what is happening: *You are not going to die.* Breathe deeply, and take a drink of water. Ground yourself by visualizing that you are connected to Mother Earth by a cord coming down through your tailbone into the earth. Have your friend speak to you in a calm manner. Keep an object with you that is grounding, such as a rock, crystal, or something else from nature that you can hold or keep in your lap.

4. When you get to your destination, reward yourself. You worked very hard and deserve recognition for stepping into your fear.

◇ ◇ ◇

REFLECTIONS OF SELF
WE ARE ALL MIRRORS FOR EACH OTHER

When we look at other people, we see many of their qualities in innumerable and seemingly random combinations. However, what we see in the people around us is directly related to the traits that exist in us. "Like attracts like" is one of the spiritual laws of the universe: We attract individuals into our lives who mirror who we are.

Those you feel drawn to reflect your inner self back at you, and you act as a mirror for them. Simply put, when you look at others, you will very likely see what exists in you. When you observe beauty, divinity, sweetness, or light in the soul of another, you are seeing the goodness that resides in *your* soul. When you see traits in others that evoke feelings of anger, annoyance, or hatred, what is being reflected back to you are those parts of yourself that you have disowned or do not like.

Since we are all mirrors for each other, looking at the people in your life can tell you a lot about yourself. Who you are can be revealed to you through what you see in others. It is easy to notice the traits you do not like in those around you. It is much more difficult to realize that *you* possess the same traits. Often the habits, attitudes, and behaviors of others are closely linked to *your* unconscious and unresolved issues.

When you come into contact with someone you admire, search your soul for similarly admirable attributes. Likewise, when you meet someone exhibiting traits that you dislike, accept that you are viewing your reflection. Looking at yourself through your perception of others can be a humbling and eye-opening experience. You can also cultivate in yourself the characteristics and behaviors that you *do* like. Be loving and respectful to all people and you will attract individuals who will love and respect you back. Nurture compassion and empathy, and let the goodness you see in others be your mirror.

◇ ◇ ◇

LIFE

YOUR PERFECT TEACHER

Many of us long to find a spiritual teacher or guru. We may feel unsure of how to practice our spirituality without one, or we may long for someone who has attained a higher level of insight to lead the way for us. Some of us have been looking for years to no avail and feel frustrated and even lost. The good news is that the greatest teacher we could ever want is always with us — our life.

The people and situations we encounter every day have much to teach us when we are open to receiving their wisdom. Often we do not recognize our instructors because they may not look or act like our idea of a guru . . . yet they may embody great wisdom. In addition, some people guide us by showing us what we *don't* want to do. All the situations in our lives, from the insignificant to the major, conspire to teach us exactly what we need to learn at any given time.

Patience, compassion, perseverance, honesty, letting go—all these are covered in the classroom of the teacher that is your life. You can help yourself remember this perfect teacher every day with a few simple words. Each morning you might find a moment to say, "I acknowledge and honor the teacher that is my life. May I be wise enough to recognize the teachers and lessons I encounter today, and may I be open to receiving their wisdom."

You might also take some time each day to consider what your life is trying to tell you at this juncture. A difficult phase in your relationship with your child could be teaching you to let go. The homeless person you see every day may be showing you the boundaries of your compassion and generosity. A spate of lost items might be asking you to be more present to physical reality. Trust your intuition on the nature of the lesson at hand, work at your own pace, and ask as many questions as you want. Your life has all the answers.

◇ ◇ ◇

THE ROAD TO NEW BEGINNINGS
COMPLETION

Life is a work of art in progress made up of beginnings and endings that run together like wet paint. Yet before we can begin any new phase in life, we must sometimes first achieve closure with respect to the current stage we are in.

Many of life's experiences call for closure. Often we cannot see the significance of an event or the importance of a lesson until we have reached it. Or we may have finished a certain phase in life or path of learning and want to honor that ending. It is this sense of completion that frees us to open the door to new beginnings. Closure serves to tie up or sever loose ends, quiets the mind even when questions have been left unanswered, signifies the conclusion of an experience, and acknowledges that a change has taken place.

The period of completion, rather than being just an act of finality, is also one of transition. When we seek closure, what we really want is an understanding of what has happened and an opportunity to derive the lessons we can from an experience. Without it, there is no resolution and we are left to grieve, relive old memories to the point of frustration, or remain forever connected to people from our past. A sense of completion regarding a situation may also result when we accept that we have done our best.

If you cannot officially achieve closure with someone, you can create a sense of completion by participating in a closure ritual. Write a farewell letter to that person and then burn your note during a ceremony. This ritual allows you to consciously honor and appreciate what has taken place between you and release the experience so that you can move forward.

Closure can help you let go of feelings of anger or uncertainty related to your past even as you honor your experience—whether good or bad—as a necessary step on your life's path. This allows you to emotionally lay to rest issues and feelings that may be weighing down your spirit. When you create closure, you affirm that you have done what was needed, are wiser because of your experience, and are ready for whatever life wants to bring you next.

◇ ◇ ◇

INSIGHTFUL ILLUMINATIONS
CANDLE MEDITATION

A lot of people like the idea of meditation, but it intimidates them. You may be one of these individuals, who think, *I can't shut off my brain . . . I can't sit still . . . I'll look like a fool . . . what will my friends think?* . . . These are all normal responses that keep people from trying meditation. But this activity is not just for mystical individuals in faraway lands. It is, in its simplest form, a method to better your focus and concentration; reduce tension, anxiety, and stress; and promote creativity and improved performance in work and play. It requires no special clothing or equipment (except, in the following case, a candle).

Here is a genuinely easy way to start a practice of daily meditation — especially for those who think they cannot do it:

1. Pick a place in your home where you will not be disturbed.

2. Try to make the atmosphere as quiet as possible, turning off phones, radios, and televisions.

3. Find a comfortable place to sit where you can set a candle at least one foot in front of you at eye level. This may require you to be seated on the floor on a cushion, perhaps with the candle on your coffee table or altar if you have one.

4. Light the candle and take three deep breaths.

5. Set your intention that at this time you will begin your meditation.

6. Start to focus your eyes on the candle flame. Watch it flicker, dance, and change color.

7. Try now to concentrate only on the flame, clearing your mind. Thoughts will come into your head—bills to pay, places to be—just let them drift into your mind and imagine them floating on a cloud passing by.

8. You may feel that you want to close your eyes after a while, and that is fine. Just keep breathing and letting the thoughts drift by.

You will know when you are done. Maybe you will feel finished after 10 minutes, or 20, but you will sense it. It is always nice to give gratitude, such as a few words of thanks, before gently blowing out your candle.

◇ ◇ ◇

OVER AND OVER AGAIN
HAVING THE SAME EXPERIENCES

There may be times in our lives when it seems as if we keep having the same kinds of experiences. The situation or the people involved may be different each time, yet one encounter may feel exactly like the last and the one before that. Perhaps we left a job where we were unhappy, and we find ourselves facing similar challenges in our current position. A relationship with a new romantic partner may start to seem a lot like our old one, and the problems resemble those we thought we had left behind.

We may feel disappointed or frustrated and wonder why the same situations and people keep showing up in our lives. The truth is that the identical experiences do not keep happening *to* us—after all, the circumstances and the individuals involved are always different. *We* simply keep having the same kinds of experiences.

Subconsciously, there is great value to be had in going through life in the same ways until we are ready to have

93

different experiences. Perhaps we feel unworthy of happiness or worry that we cannot get a break. Our lives tend to reflect what we believe about them. After all, most of us do not like to be proven wrong. We may even derive satisfaction in being right or gain a sense of safety every time we confirm to ourselves that we know the way the world works. We may choose a relationship partner who is very different from our last significant other and hope that this time love will turn out differently. Despite this, as long as we hold those beliefs that restrict the good we can experience in our relationships, we will create the identical dynamic of limited happiness with *any* partner.

We bring ourselves and our beliefs to every situation. If we can figure out which of those convictions no longer serve us, we can consciously change them, make fresh choices, and start having new kinds of experiences that are in line with what we want in life.

◇ ◇ ◇

SPIRITUALIZING THE PLANET
ASCENSION

We are one with the cosmos whether we realize it or not. Realizing it, though, quickens our spiritual energy and allows us access to higher realms. In these realms lies the awareness that we are more than just finite physical beings living one life in one place at one point in time. To connect with this awareness is to awaken to the truth and take a step forward, and upward, on our soul's journey. This movement is known as *ascension,* because the more we remember who we are and embody that truth, the higher our energy vibrates; we ascend the scale from the gross physical plane to the subtle spiritual one. As we do so, we gain consciousness of the more subtle aspects of our being, the ultimate outcome of which is a complete identification with the light body — an experience of unification with the cosmos.

As you look around you, you will see that many people are not even interested in these ideas, some are open and paying attention, while still others have devoted their lives to deepening their understanding of the truth. All these people are on the path of ascension, but they will ascend at different rates. The last group are at the forefront of an important process of raising the energetic vibration of the whole planet.

Each soul chooses its own way. The more devoted a person is to remembering and being guided by spirit, the more quickly the soul will ascend. The earth, made of the same energy that we are, is undergoing this shift along with us. This evolutionary process, while seemingly chaotic at times, is as natural as the process that transforms a flower from a seed, and we are all part of it.

It should not be forgotten that the earth, too, is on her own ascension path, as she is sentient. The best way to support this process in yourself and in the world is simply to relax and be open to its unfolding. Listen to your inner guidance and let it direct you to the path that brings your heart the most joy.

◇ ◇ ◇

WORKING FROM CENTER
IN THE THICK OF IT

When we are in the thick of it, overwhelmed by too many things that need our attention, it is important to remember that we are never given more than we can handle. When life's challenges make us question this, our best coping mechanism is to follow the reliable and well-known course to our calm center, and anchor ourselves there. It is for these times that we have been practicing regularly so that our mind, body, and spirit will know how to find the peace within. Even in the midst of seeming chaos, a deep breath can help us turn within to find the space to work from: the calm at the center of the storm.

Tapping into our inner resources, we begin again, bringing our focus to the needs of the present moment. Asking "Why?" shifts our energy away from the task at hand. We can seek answers to those questions once we get to the other side of the current challenge. For now, we accept what is.

Once we have collected scattered energy and have created space, inspiration will strike, help will arrive, and what seemed impossible either will become possible or we will find that it has become unnecessary. The flow of the universe and its perfect order has room to move in our lives when we get ourselves and our extraneous thoughts out of the way.

After the thick has become thin again, we have the opportunity to learn from the situation with a better idea of our true capabilities. We can now ask ourselves the "Why?" questions with the goal of fine-tuning our lives. Perhaps we have taken on more than is ours to do or made commitments out of obligation rather than insight. It could just be the ebb and flow of life, or we may be receiving life lessons on a fast track in preparation for something wonderful to come. But when we have a chance to make new choices, we know the best ones come when we work from center.

◇ ◇ ◇

ASKING FOR WHAT YOU WANT
CO-CREATING WITH THE UNIVERSE

Most people do not always fully realize that we all have within us the ability to co-create our lives with the universe. So many of us are taught to accept what we are given and not dream of anything more, but our hopes and aspirations are the universe whispering to us, planting an idea of what is possible while directing us toward the best use of our gifts. The universe truly wants to give us our hearts' desires, but we need to be clear about what they are and ask for them.

To ask for something does not mean to beg or plead from a place of lack or unworthiness. It is like placing an order: We do not need to beg the salespeople for what we want or prove to them that we deserve to have it—it is their job to give us what we request; we only have to *tell* them. Once we have a clear vision of what we desire, we simply step into the silent realm where all possibilities exist and let our desires be known. Whatever methods we use, it is important that we find the quiet space between our thoughts.

From that still and silent place, we can announce our intentions to the pure energy of creation. By imagining all the details from every angle—including scent, color, and how it would feel to have our wishes fulfilled—we design our dreams to our specifications. Similar to dropping a pebble into a pond, the ripples created by our thoughts travel quickly from this place of stillness, echoing out into the world to align and orchestrate all the necessary details to bring our desires into manifestation. Before leaving this wonderful space to come back to the world, we must release any attachment to the outcome and express gratitude. By doing this daily, we focus our thoughts and energy while regularly mingling with the essence that makes it possible to build the life of our dreams.

◇ ◇ ◇

MOVING INTO A NEW PHASE
OUTGROWING FRIENDS

Every one of us lives a life colored by individual and changing experiences, perceptions, needs, and desires. We connect with others, becoming friends and confidants, most often because they share something with us, such as an interest or need. As time goes on, there is change, and the bonds that brought us close to a treasured friend may not be enough to sustain the relationship. We may find that our lives have gone in wildly different directions and we no longer share the same aspirations, or we may have shifted on an energetic level.

It is not unusual in such situations to discover that the comfort you found in the other person has vanished and that you have trouble relating as you once did. Outgrowing a friend can be confusing or painful, but it is a natural part of your personal growth.

You have a right to choose to surround yourself with those people who understand you, are helpful and compassionate, and put you at ease. Months or years into a friendship, you may find that your friend no longer seems like the same person he or she once was. The change may have been within the other person, but it could also have come from within *you*. Moving on does not mean that your past shared experiences were not meaningful or important to you both; rather, it acknowledges your needs in the present.

Ending a friendship can be difficult. You may not feel comfortable explaining your reasons for doing so. Even so, you can still be kind, respectful, and considerate and simply state that you can no longer devote time to the friendship. When you have made the conscious decision to let go of the relationship, it will most likely happen naturally.

Each person who has been a part of your life taught you something. Some friendships are long-term, while others are brief. In all relationships, however, it is important to embrace changes and let go of regrets. While you may outgrow the need to maintain a bond with someone who was once very special to you, that person will nonetheless always occupy a place in your heart.

◇ ◇ ◇

FLUID LIKE A RIVER
LIVING LIKE WATER

The journey of water as it flows upon the earth can be a mirror of our own paths through life. Water begins its residence on Earth as it falls from the sky or melts from ice and cascades down a mountain into a tributary or stream. In the same way, we come into the world and begin our lives on Earth. Like a river that flows within the confines of its banks, we are born with certain defining characteristics that govern our identity. We are born in a particular time and place, into a specific family, and with certain gifts and challenges. Within these parameters, we move through life, encountering many twists, turns, and obstacles along the way—just as a river flows.

Water is a great teacher that shows us how to move through the world with grace, ease, determination, and humility. When a river breaks at a waterfall, it gains energy and moves on. As we encounter our own waterfalls, we may fall hard, but we always keep going. Water can inspire us not to become rigid with fear or hold fast to what is familiar. Water is brave and does not waste time clinging to its past but flows onward without looking back. At the same time, when there is a hole to be filled, water does not flee from it, fearful of the dark; instead, it humbly and bravely fills the empty space. In the same way, we can face the dark moments of life rather than running away from them.

Eventually, a river will empty into the sea. Water does not hold back from joining with a larger body, nor does it fear a loss of identity or control. It gracefully and humbly tumbles into the vastness by contributing its energy and merging without resistance. Each time we move beyond our individual egos to become part of something bigger, we can try our best to follow the lead of the river.

◇ ◇ ◇

SPREADING HAPPINESS
SMILING

The face is a complex palette of emotions. A slight turning up of the lips and a crinkling of the eyes can signal pleasure, contentment, happiness, or satisfaction. In all cases, a smile is more than it seems. A grinning person is often judged more attractive, pleasant to be around, sincere, honest, sociable, and inviting, and is considered more confident and successful. Smiling is not a learned action. Even those born blind will have this facial expression when experiencing a joyful moment. A carefree smile is a quick and easy way to tell the world that you are open to new experiences and eager to meet new people.

It is assumed that bright smiles stem from happiness, but research has also shown that genuine joy can stem from *them*. Even a smile called forth when you do not necessarily feel like smiling can trigger the release of endorphins, brightening your day. This simple act can help relieve stress by relaxing your facial muscles and encouraging you to focus on happy memories. And a forced smile, which only involves the muscles of the mouth, can easily turn into a true one, which lights up the entire face. A smile motivated by real happiness is likely to inspire someone nearby to imitate it, possibly because of the expression's origins in the primate grin. That grin, which some scientists believe evolved into the smile, signaled that its wearer was a friend rather than an opponent.

In ancient China, Taoists taught the benefits of the inner smile because they believed it ensured happiness, health, and longevity. A single smile can lessen the sting of a negative mood and bring on a better one. But try not to be self-conscious about it—this expression is universal and looks great on everyone. A smile, directed inward, outward, or at nothing in particular, uplifts the world and is a gift to those who see it.

◇ ◇ ◇

LIVING POTENTIAL
SHARING YOUR GIFTS WITH OTHERS

The gifts we are born with and those we work to develop throughout our lives vary in form and function. Some we find use for every day, while others are only of value in specific circumstances. Many times we overlook opportunities to share our unique gifts with others. It may be fear of criticism that holds us back or the paralyzing weight of uncertainty. Ultimately, we doubt that our innate talents and practiced skills can truly add to others' lives, but it is the world as a whole that benefits when we willingly share our gifts.

Whether you have been blessed with the ability to awaken beautiful emotions in others through art or industry or your aptitudes transmit more practical advantages, your gifts are a part of who you are. As you make use of them as best you can, be assured that your contribution to global well-being will not be overlooked.

Your personal power is defined in part by your gifts. To use your talents is to demonstrate to the world that you understand yourself and are truly attuned to your capabilities. Your earthly existence provides you with ample opportunity to explore your purpose, to utilize your skills in a life-affirming way, and to positively touch the lives of others while doing so. You may feel that your gifts are not as valuable or worthy of attention as those of others, and hide them away. However, every one that's lying dormant in your soul has the potential to fill a void in someone else's life. Just as your existence is made richer by the love, support, friendship, aid, and compassion of others, so, too, can you add richness to *their* lives. Your natural ability to soothe hurt, inspire compassion, bake, dance, knit, organize, or think outside the box can be a boon to someone in need.

As you embrace your gifts and allow their light to shine, you will discover that more and more opportunities to make use of them arise. This is because your gifts are a channel through which the universe operates. By simply doing what you are good at and love to do, you make a positive difference. The recognition you receive for your efforts will pale in comparison to the satisfaction you feel when fulfilling your innate potential.

◇ ◇ ◇

REINVENTING THE PAST
HEALING YOUR INNER CHILD

As we tread our individual pathways in life, we can acquire what some refer to as *emotional baggage*. Much of it is easy to recognize, but that which was picked up when we were very young is often hidden deep within the subconscious. The inner child or child within can harbor decades of old hurt that can cause us to react to situations and people using childhood pain as a template.

This means that sometimes your reactions have less to do with the situation at hand and more to do with things you experienced long ago but have not forgotten. The inner child is an important piece of your emotional makeup. It can be playful, spontaneous, intuitive, and spiritual—but it can also be fearful, distrustful, and critical. Painful childhood experiences can negatively affect adult ones. Healing the inner child addresses your child-self's wounds and frees your grown-up self to make decisions based on the present.

There are steps you can take to gently begin healing your inner child. Working with this hidden part of you is very much like solving a mystery, and the first step to unlocking it is analyzing your own behavior:

1. Ask yourself why you are attracted to certain people; why you react the way you do in particular situations; and what makes you feel helpless, scared, angry, or lonely. As you do so, remember that there is nothing wrong with your feelings and no shame in being influenced by your inner child.

2. Inquire of yourself how those feelings have been shaped by past experiences. Then mentally revisit your childhood. Visualize yourself as you were when you were young. Feel what your child self is feeling.

3. Finally, approach him or her and offer comfort in the form of a hug infused with positive, loving energy. In doing so, you are both healing and letting go of the wounded child's pain.

Attempting to discount the fact that the inner child has an effect on the adult denies the impact of old wounds and past experiences. Acknowledging this part of you honors your former self and can help you recover painful memories that have been repressed. However, recalling specific ones is not vital to healing. It is enough to be aware that you can change the way you unconsciously learned to react in your youth by nurturing your inner child and, in doing so, foster a loving and wise present self.

◇ ◇ ◇

HAVING vs. NOT HAVING

LACK

We all know what it feels like to want something we do not have. It may be a pair of expensive jeans, a romantic partner, or rent money; it may be a certain attitude, a car, or a savings account. This is part of life; and in the best-case scenario, we experience a constant flow of money, companions, and experiences in and out of our lives. However, many of us linger in a state of wanting and not having, a condition of lack that never seems to subside. We consistently perceive ourselves as not having what we need or not having what we want. This is an energetically draining state to be in. It is also self-perpetuating, because the way we feel about ourselves determines what we are able to create for ourselves.

How we feel profoundly influences how we perceive our reality. When we believe that we are lacking, we look around and see what is not there. On the other hand, if we feel abundant, we can look at the very same situation and see a completely different picture, one full of blessings and advantages. The more we see the blessings, the more abundant we feel, and the more blessings we attract. Similarly, if we see lack, we tend to create and attract that energy.

If you find yourself habitually residing in a feeling of "not enough," it may be due to a core belief formed in your childhood or even in a past life. It could be because you are out of touch with your inner divinity, which is the source of your abundance. In any case, know that your perception of lack is a *mis*perception that can be corrected with awareness and effort. It may be as simple as taking 10 or 15 minutes each day to quiet your mind and imagine yourself in a state of unlimited plenitude, handling the financial demands and other people in your life with total ease, drawing from an endless supply of resources. Know that it is your birthright to be fully supported in the fulfillment of your needs and desires.

◇ ◇ ◇

GUT RESPONSE
IN TOUCH WITH TRUE EMOTIONS

So often emotions we long to express get stored in our bodies instead. The space where this most often happens is our bellies. Rather than telling people, or even ourselves, the way we truly feel, we may stuff our true feelings deep inside of us, where they take up space until we are ready to let them go. Holding our feelings in our abdomen may feel like the safe response, since we do not really have to deal with them, but doing so can actually be detrimental to our emotional well-being and physical health.

One way to connect with and release your emotions is to do a focused exercise with your abdominal area. Take a moment to center yourself with some deep breathing and quiet meditation, relaxing your body fully and turning off the chatter in your brain. With your right hand on your belly, tell yourself three times: "Please reveal to me my true emotions."

Listen for the answers. Repeat the exercise as many times as you would like, allowing yourself to drop deeper into your body each time. Notice any physical response in the abdominal area, whether you have a warm, relaxed feeling in the middle of your body or feel tight knots in response to whatever emotions come up. You may even want to write down any answers that come to you. Remember that the body does not lie.

Releasing your pent-up feelings from your belly can prevent disease and allow you to live a more authentic and expressive life. Sometimes if too much emotional energy builds up inside, a blowout can result and cause discomfort. You can help alleviate this compression by doing the same exercise and adding sound to your emotional release. The more guttural the noises emitted through your mouth, the more emotions you are likely letting go. Releasing your emotions from your belly does not have to be painful and hard; rather, it can be organic and effortless. It is important not to judge whatever comes up for you.

We tend to stuff our feelings in our bellies when we are ashamed of them or are not ready to express them. There is nothing wrong with having them, whatever they may be. You cannot help it; if anything, you can help yourself by acknowledging the *truth* of your emotions so that you can set yourself free.

◇ ◇ ◇

YOUR OWN SUBVERSION
OVERCOMING SELF-SABOTAGE

Each one of us is blessed with the ability to want. Some desire to achieve financial success, some to change the world, and others simply to change themselves for the better. Each one of us also has the power to make what we want a reality. Often, however, we subtly undermine our efforts by refusing support, adopting an air of ambivalence, over-committing, being indecisive, or listening to our doubts. This is self-sabotage.

Sometimes it is not a deficiency of desire, intelligence, skill, or effort that is holding you back, but an internal tug-of-war based on fear. You know what you want from life but consciously, or *sub*consciously, get in the way of your efforts. There is a conflict between your desires and your feelings of worth and entitlement.

Self-sabotaging behavior can affect your motivation and your drive. You may drown your strong desires in television or food, avoid facing potentially challenging situations, or simply retreat inward. Accepting challenges, growing, making tough decisions, and working hard can seem truly frightening. It is easier to continue doing what you have always done. But the more you turn away from the means to achieve your life's dreams, the more your self-esteem and confidence is damaged. In that way, self-sabotage is cyclical: You shy away from going after what you want and then believe that you lack the *ability* to get it.

Self-sabotage can inspire feelings of depression, frustration, discouragement, and even anger because you are working against yourself. If you feel you have hindered your own efforts, remember and write down times when you did so. Do not use the information to judge yourself. Instead, try to avoid similarly sabotaging yourself in the future.

Recognize that all worthwhile goals take patience, organization, work, and a measure of confidence. Self-sabotage nearly always comes from feelings of inadequacy or undeservedness, but those feelings can be overcome by giving yourself an extra portion of nurturing and love when you are working out a problem or formulating a long-term plan. All desires are special and valid, and learning to overcome self-sabotage is an important part of achieving what you want.

◇ ◇ ◇

PEOPLE WHO DON'T GET IT
COMPASSION FOR ALL

You may be someone who understands the true nature of reality, perceiving deeply that we all emanate from the same source, that we are all essentially one, and that we are here on Earth to love one another. To understand this is to be awakened to the true nature of the self, and this under-standing is a blessing. Nevertheless, people who just do not get it are seemingly everywhere and, often, occupy positions of power. It can be frustrating and painful to watch them behave unconsciously.

We all encounter individuals such as these in our families, at work, and in all areas of public life. It is easy to find ourselves feeling intolerant of these people, wishing we could be free of them even though we know that separation from them is an illusion.

It helps sometimes to think of us all as different parts of one psyche. Within our own hearts and minds we have dark places that need healing, just as the heart and mind of the world have *their* dark places. The health of the whole organism depends upon the relative health of the individuals within it. We increase harmony when we hold on to the light, not allowing it to be clouded by judgment, anger, and fear about those who behave unconsciously. It is easier to accomplish this if we don't focus on the negative qualities of individuals and instead on how increasing our own light will increase that of the overall picture.

When dealing with people who seem very unconscious, it helps to remember that everyone must find their own way to awakening, and that the experience they are having is an essential part of their process. Holding them in the glow of *our* energy may be the best way to awaken *theirs*. At the same time, we are inspired by their example to look within and shed light on our own unconscious places, sacrificing the urge to judge and surrendering instead to humble self-inquiry.

◇ ◇ ◇

THOUGHTS OF CONCERN
WHEN WORRY BECOMES A PRAYER

If prayer is an intention that we announce to the universe in order to create a desired outcome, then our *every* thought is a prayer. This includes those of worry as well as of hope—*all* are subtle creative energy. Some thoughts are more focused or repeated more often, gathering strength. Some are written down or spoken, giving them even greater power. Every one that we have is part of a process whereby we co-create our experience and our reality with the universe. When we use our creative energy unconsciously, we invoke what is commonly known as a self-fulfilling prophecy. In essence, when we worry, we are repeatedly praying and lending our energy to the creation of something we do not want.

The good news is that we can retrain our minds and thoughts to focus our energy on what we *do* desire to bring into our lives. Since most worry is repetitive, it will take more than one positive thought to counteract the force we have created. The simplest antidote to anxiety is affirmations. When we hold these uplifting thoughts, repeat them often, speak them, write them, and refer to them throughout our day, we are using focused energy to manifest positive results.

We can start right away together:

*"I am a creative being, using my energy to co-create
a wonderful world. I know that I create my experience of life
from within, and as I do so, I also send forth ripples of energy
around me that echo into the world. My positive thoughts gather
with the thoughts and prayers of others, and together we create
enough positive energy not only to heal our own lives, but
also the earth we share. I am grateful for the ability
to co-create good in my life and on the planet."*

A lot of times we have concerned loved ones who worry about us. When this occurs, they are also sending out a worry prayer to the world. A loving conversation letting them know what is happening is the easiest solution. Also, ask them to send you positive affirmations rather than fretting about you. After all, worry does not do them any good either. Explain to them that it can actually be energetically harmful to you, and that wishing good things for you is much more beneficial—and much more fun, too.

◇ ◇ ◇

GOING THROUGH THE OPENING
CONTRACTING BEFORE EXPANDING

Sometimes our lives contract before they expand. We may be working hard on ourselves spiritually, doing good in the world, following our dreams, and wondering why we are still facing constrictions of all kinds—financial, emotional, physical, and so on. Perhaps we even feel as if we have lost our spirituality and are stuck in a dark room with no windows. We may be confused and discouraged by what appears to be a lack of progress. Sometimes this is simply the way things work. Like a caterpillar that confines itself to a tiny cocoon before it grows wings and flies, we are experiencing the darkness before the light.

When things feel tight, it is easy to panic or to want to act to somehow ease the sense of constriction. We might also spin our wheels mentally, trying to understand why things are the way they are. However, there is nothing we need to do at this time other than be patient and persevering. We can cling to the awareness that we are processing the shift from one stage to another, and the more we surrender to the experience, the more quickly we will move through the tightness and into the opening on the other side. Just like a baby making its way down the birth canal, we may feel squeezed and pushed and very uncomfortable, but if we remember that we are on our way to being born into a new reality, we will find the strength to carry on.

Even as we endure the contracting, we can find peace within ourselves if we remember to have faith in the universe. We are able to look to the natural world for inspiration as we see that all beings surrender to the process of being born. In that surrender, and in the center of our own hearts, is a willingness to trust in the unknown.

◇ ◇ ◇

AGAINST THE GRAIN
GOING AGAINST WHAT IS POPULAR

Just because an idea or manner of doing things is popular does not mean that it is right for everyone. However, part of the way something *becomes* popular is that many of us do not take the time to *determine* what is right for us; we simply do what most of the people we know are doing. In this way, our decisions about life are made by default, which means that they are not what we call "conscious."

There may be many other options available, but we do not always take the time to explore them. This could be the result of feeling overwhelmed or pressured by family, peers, and humanity at large to do things "their" way—the way they have always been done. Regardless of the cause, it is important that, as often as we can, we decide for ourselves what to do with our lives rather than just drifting along on the current of popular opinion.

It is not always easy to make decisions that go against the grain. Many people feel threatened when the choices of those close to them diverge from the ones they are making. Parents and grandparents may be confused and defensive when we opt to raise our children differently from the way they raised us. Friends may feel abandoned if we decide to change our habits or behavior. Meanwhile, on *our* side of the fence, it is easy to be frustrated and defensive when we feel unsupported and misunderstood simply because we are thinking for ourselves. It can be exhausting to have to explain and reexplain our points of view and our reasons.

This is where gentleness, openness, and tolerance come into play. It helps if we are calmly persistent, consistent, and clear as we communicate to those around us why we are making the choices that we are. At the same time, we have the right to say that we are tired of talking about it and simply need our choices to be respected. Our lives belong to us, and so do our decisions. Those who truly love us will stand by us and support them—never mind what is popular.

◇ ◇ ◇

EMPTINESS BECOMES OPENNESS
SOMETIMES A LOSS CAN BE A GAIN

When we lose anything that we cherish, the sense of emptiness we are left with can be overwhelming. A space that was filled, whether in our lives or our hearts, is now a void; and the feelings of pain, loss, and separation can sometimes be difficult to bear. While it is always important to honor what we have lost, sometimes this can also represent a chance for a new beginning. When we are ready, the vacancy left by a relationship, a job, or a dream can then be viewed as open space that can be filled with something new: experiences, knowledge, job opportunities, dreams, people, and ways to grow.

There are many methods to weave the threads of loss into a blessing. If you have lost a job or ended a relationship, your first thoughts may revolve around filling the void with similar work or the same kind of relationship. Try not to rush into anything just to fill up the emptiness.

The loss of a job can free you up to explore new opportunities, especially if you have outgrown the old one. Likewise, the end of a relationship can give you a chance to rediscover your own interests, explore new passions, and meet different people.

If seeking the good in what seems like a bad situation makes you feel uncomfortable, then try to remember that you are not devaluing what you have lost or replacing it coldheartedly. You are surrendering to the fact that in life we sometimes have to let go and allow what is new to enter into the vacant spaces created by our losses. In doing so, you are honoring what has left you and welcoming the new into your life with open space, an open mind, and an open heart.

◇ ◇ ◇

POTENTIAL OF GROWTH
SEEDS FOR LIVING

When we look at a giant sequoia tree, it is hard to imagine that it grew from a tiny seed no bigger than a flake of oatmeal. Conversely, to hold such a small thing as a seed in our hands and comprehend that contained within it is the blueprint for an entire forest of trees that will surpass the human life span by centuries is enough to stun the mind into silence. As tiny as that seed is, *we* are somehow even more so.

Yet, we are grown seeds in our own right, originating in our mothers' wombs in a form too small to be seen with the naked eye, imbued with the same miraculous life force as sequoias. We drop our own seeds, in the form of children or creative projects, which go on after we pass from the earth, and a part of us continues with them.

The environment in which seeds grow also influences them. A tree on a windswept mountain will have longer branches in the direction the wind blows. A houseplant will grow toward the window where the light comes in. The type of plant grown is in the seed, but the shape it takes is due to its environment. Similarly, we are the products of both our genetic material and the sort of nurturing we received during childhood. At the same time, we are always in the process of growth. Now it is up to us to provide the right surroundings for ourselves.

A lovely ritual to perform as an act of self-love is to plant a bulb or a seed in a pot and allow it to be a symbol of your intention to nurture yourself. Remember that you were once smaller than that tiny seed. Honor how amazing you are to have gotten as far as you have. Plant a piece of paper in the soil stating your intention to provide yourself with everything you need now to continue to grow strong and beautiful. Each time you water the seed, talk to it, or move it to a more beneficial location, you are honoring and fostering your own expansion.

◇ ◇ ◇

WHERE YOU NEED TO BE
TIMING CAN BE EVERYTHING

Since human timetables quite often do not correspond with universal ones, it is common for people to feel that life is progressing too slowly or too quickly. We draft carefully composed plans, only to find that they fall into place when we least expect them to. Or, conversely, we are thrust into roles that we believe we are not prepared for and wonder how we will survive the demands imposed upon us by unfamiliar circumstances. When delays in our progress kindle pangs of disappointment within us or the pace of life seems overwhelming, peace can be found in the simple fact that we are exactly where we need to be at this moment.

Every person fulfills their purpose when the time is right. If you have fast-tracked your way to success, you may become deeply frustrated if you discover that you can no longer satisfy your desires as quickly as you might like. But the delays that disappoint you may be laying the foundation for future accomplishments that you have not yet conceived of. Or the universe may have plans for you that differ from the worldly aspirations you have pursued up until this point. What you deem a postponement of progress may actually represent an auspicious opportunity to prepare for what is to come.

If, however, you feel as though the universe is pushing you forward at too fast a clip, you may be unwittingly resisting your destiny. Your unease regarding the speed of your progress could be a sign that you need to cultivate awareness within yourself and learn to move *with* the flow of fate rather than against it. The universe puts nothing in your path that you are incapable of handling, so you can rest assured that you are ready to grow into your new situation.

You may feel compelled to judge your personal success using your age, your professional position, your level of education, or the achievements of your peers as a yardstick. We all enjoy the major milestones in our lives at the appropriate time; some realize their dreams as youngsters, while others flourish only in old age. If you take pride in your many accomplishments and make the most of every circumstance in which you find yourself, your time will come.

◇ ◇ ◇

OPENING TO FEEL
WAYS WE NUMB OURSELVES

We are born equipped to experience a complex array of diverse emotions. Many of us, however, are uncomfortable confronting our most powerful emotions. We may shy away from delight and despair and deny life's colors by retreating into a world of monochrome gray. We may numb ourselves to what we are truly feeling. It is easier to suppress our emotions than to deal with them, so we may momentarily turn to pleasures such as alcohol, food, sugar, shopping, and too much television. We may even numb our hearts.

While it is normal to temporarily seek distractions as a means of coping with intense emotions, numbing yourself prevents you from confronting your issues and keeps you from ever finding resolution or peace. When you are in this state, there is no pain or powerlessness, but there can also be no joy or healing.

The activities that numb you may seem harmless or pleasurable, but using them to dull your senses diminishes the quality of your life. Numbing yourself so that you do not have to feel intense emotions can often satisfy a surface need while blocking your awareness of a deeper emotion. You may find solace in food or shopping when what you really need is spiritual nourishment. The less you feel, the less *alive* you are. Your feelings add vividness to your experiences and serve to connect you to the world around you.

It is possible to divest yourself of numbing habits a little at a time and once again taste life's rich flavors. When you sense that you are engaging in a particular behavior simply to deaden your emotions, stop and ask yourself why. Examining the feelings that drive you to do so can help you understand what is triggering your desire to emotionally fade out.

With each numbing activity that you cut out of your life, you will find yourself being more aware and experiencing a greater emotional acuity. Senses once shrouded by the fog of numbness become sharp and keen. Traumas and pain long hidden will emerge to the forefront of your consciousness and reveal themselves so that you can heal them. You will discover a deeper you, a self that is comfortable experiencing and working through intense emotions with courage and grace.

◇ ◇ ◇

REACHING OUT
ASKING FOR HELP

We like to be helpful. We volunteer at schools, shelters, and food banks. We give millions each year to charitable organizations. On a more intimate level, we make chicken soup for sick friends, dog-sit for our neighbors, and even stop to help strangers with car trouble.

Yet many of us are reluctant to solicit aid when we need it. Any number of reasons may keep us from reaching out and asking for or even accepting assistance. Pride, embarrassment, not wanting to be an imposition, or fear of rejection can prevent us from seeking help, even when we very well may be in need.

Needing help is not a weakness. It may be a challenge and a risk to ask for it, but that gives us one more opportunity to grow and learn. Reaching out to others teaches us many things about ourselves. Requesting aid requires examining our own needs and accepting areas where there is room for improvement in our lives. We are called to put aside our egos and admit that we are not totally self-sufficient.

There is certainly no shame in requiring assistance setting up a new computer or asking someone to hem a pair of pants. There are times when we may need even more help — for instance, someone to drive us to the doctor, lend us money for an emergency, or talk to us when we are down. When we ask for help, we come to understand that we all need each other, and allowing others to help us offers an opportunity for our family and friends — and even strangers — to feel useful and appreciated. As we want to be helpful, so, too, do others.

Reaching out for assistance teaches us to trust. Whether we call upon people, animals, angels, and/or the universe, we can believe our needs will be answered. We are always reminded that there is compassion and that we are loved and cared for.

Think of the ways you could use a little help in your life, and reach out and ask. Let someone be of service to you today. Give and the world gives back. Allow that to happen.

◇ ◇ ◇

THOSE WHO CAME BEFORE
TURNING TO ANCESTORS FOR GUIDANCE

Many entities assume the role of spirit guides. Throughout our lives, we may call upon angels, animal and nature spirits, ascended masters, and celestial guardians for aid, protection, and support. Our ancestors represent another wellspring from which we may draw wisdom in times of need, for they, too, can act as our spirit guides. Since our forebears spent at least one lifetime experiencing the tribulations that are a part of human existence, the perspective they can offer is a uniquely grounded one. They can empathize with our fears; frailties; and feelings of insecurity, worry, and temptation.

Once you have requested their guidance, ancestral spirit guides will see to it that you emerge unscathed on the far side of conflicts and are well equipped to fulfill your potential. If your relationship with your relatives was strained when they were earthbound or you feel disconnected from your heritage, the thought of asking your ancestors for aid can be disconcerting. But when the soul takes on its spirit form, it becomes pure light. Your ancestors, regardless of who or what they were when they were alive, are monitoring your life's journey because you are their progeny, and they want to see you do your best.

You can communicate with them directly, as well as through meditation, your dreams, or the written word. Creating an altar or shrine that displays images of your forebears or objects owned by them can help you connect with individual ancestors. The guidance they provide may take many forms, as each ancestral spirit guide retains its individual identity and will thus have its own style of communication. If yours do not speak to you directly or visit you in your dreams, examine your life to determine whether they are replying to your queries subconsciously.

When you make contact with your ancestors, thank them for being a part of the web of intent that gave you life. Honoring their wisdom and experience can make your life seem larger and richer. Like other spirit guides, your forebears will not interfere with your choices or attempt to deprive you of free will. They will only do their best to answer your questions and provide you with all the love, aid, and guidance you ask for in order to help you evolve as an individual.

◇ ◇ ◇

DAYS OF AFFIRMATION
SENDING LOVE AHEAD TO YOUR DAY

Upon waking, many people consider the coming day with trepidation. Because of the natural human tendency to focus on what we fear or dislike, it is easy to unwittingly send a message of unrest into the future that negatively impacts the quality of our day. However, while our lives are busy and frequently replete with challenges, they are also rich with joy and experiences worth savoring. We can attract this natural bliss by starting each day with a message of love.

When you send love ahead to your day, that feeling will manifest itself in your interpersonal interactions, your professional endeavors, and your domestic duties. Tasks and circumstances once made trying by your own anxiety are transformed by your caring, and you will find yourself approaching life's subtle nuances with great affection.

Each morning when you have cast off the fog of sleep, take several deep, grounding breaths and reaffirm the love

you have for yourself. Speaking a loving, self-directed blessing aloud enables you to access and awaken the reservoir of
tenderness in your soul. Before you leave the comfortable
warmth of your bed, be sure to tell the universe that you are
eager and ready to receive the blessings it has set aside for
you. Then as you prepare to meet the day, visualize yourself
first saturated, and then surrounded, with a warm and soft
loving light. Gradually widen the circle of this illumination
until you are able to send it ahead into your future.

If you are commuting to work, transmit love to the
roads upon which you will drive, your fellow commuters,
and your parking space. If you have colleagues who arrive
at your workplace before you, send them good wishes.
Likewise, a day spent being a parent or addressing house-
hold chores can benefit from the sentiment that precedes
you. Sending love ahead to everyone you will meet and
everything you will do can ensure that your day is suffused
with grace.

If you have difficulty directing love to those situations
and individuals you deem particularly frustrating, consider
that the warmth and tenderness you project can change
your life for the better. Each morning in sending this love,
you will exercise your power to control the ambience of
your existence and color your day with a positive force.

◇ ◇ ◇

INNER-HEALING WISDOM
TUNING IN TO SICKNESS

The physical body is like a biological computer: It is composed of innumerable components and stores many things in its vast memory. Although we try to rid ourselves of illnesses in the form of viruses, diseases, and aches and pains, these, too, are a part of the human computer. The mind body system is miraculous, utilizing everything in its control to send us signs. Chronic discomfort can be a sign of discord, infection may indicate exhaustion or emotional repression, and a sour stomach could signal anger or stress. Many illnesses are manifest into being through our actions or inactions, bottled-up worries, or inability to feel deserving.

Since your body will not lie to you, it is often possible to not only become well, but to treat the underlying root of the illness by tuning in to it. Essentially, it is another part of your body and, as such, can be communicated with.

If all people were to live lovingly, positively, and naturally, there would no doubt be less sickness. In this age of heavy workloads, complicated interpersonal interactions, indoor activities, and pollution, however, the body begs to be consulted when illness strikes. When you feel sickness coming on, or if you have been dealing with it for a long period, take time out of your day to sit quietly and relax deeply. When you have reached a state of intense calm, ask whatever plagues you (be it virus, bacteria, or pain) what it wants. Talk to it as if it were an entity within you, and have a conversation with it. It is important to listen after you have posed your question; your body has all the answers.

If nothing is immediately forthcoming, ruminate on your life of late. Are you avoiding a stressful situation or unconsciously seeking sympathy? That could be the case, but the response you receive may not necessarily be profound. It can be specific or somewhat vague. What your sickness tells you may be surprising. However, when you have acknowledged and accepted the answer, your recovery will be swift.

Tuning in to your illness can help you learn new, more effective, adaptive, and powerful ways of dealing with sickness. Putting your faith in the ability of the mind to regenerate the body, and vice versa, is an important step on the journey toward lasting self-healing.

◇ ◇ ◇

LET YOURSELF BE CARRIED
THE FLOW OF THE UNIVERSE

The flow of the universe moves through everything. It is in the rocks that form, get pounded into dust, and are blown away. It is in the blossoming of a flower born from a seed planted in the spring. The growth cycle that every human being goes through is part of this natural flow, which is also the current that takes us down life's paths. When we move with it rather than resisting it, we are riding on the universal wave that allows us to flow with life.

Many people live struggling against this current. They try to use force or resistance to will their lives into happening in the way they think it should. Others move with it like a sailor using the wind, trusting that the universe is taking them exactly where they need to be at all times. This flow is accessible to everyone because it travels through and around us. We are always riding it — it is just a matter of whether we are willing to go with it or we resist it. Choosing to go with the flow is often a matter of relinquishing the notion that we need to be in control at all times.

The flow is always transporting you where you need to go. It is merely a question of deciding whether you plan on accepting the ride or having it take you there with your feet dragging. Learning to step into it can help you feel a connection to a force that is greater than you and is always there to support you. The decision to go with the flow takes courage because you are surrendering the belief that you need to do everything by yourself. Riding the flow of the universe can be effortless, exhilarating, and unlike anything you ever expected. When you are receptive to being in it, you open yourself to possibilities that exist beyond the grasp of your control.

As a child, you were naturally swept by the flow. Tears of sadness falling down your face could just as quickly turn to tears of laughter. The mere tiniest wave carrying you forward off the shores of the ocean could transport you into peals of delight.

Our souls feel good when we go with the flow of the universe. All we have to do is make the choice to ride its currents.

◇ ◇ ◇

EARTHLY COMFORT
CONNECTING TO NATURE

Being in the midst of a redwood forest, gazing up at stars, pondering the vastness of a desert—all these nature-scapes and many more move us to a place of reverence. We connect with nature on a spiritual level. There is sacredness in wild places, and we can be transformed simply by being there.

Beyond human beings, we are *nature* beings, created from the same source as animals, plants . . . even rocks. The earth calls for us to connect so that we can feel balanced and whole—a part of the universe. Hugging a tree feels good (all jokes aside). The strength of wood is a comfort in its solidness, and we feel supported when we lean against it. It seems natural to wrap our arms around the trunk, as if the tree were hugging us back. The leaves sing to us on a breeze, reminding us that we are loved.

Being outdoors awakens all of our senses. We breathe more deeply, taking in scents of salt air, pine needles, fragrant flowers, and even the pungent odor of dirt. Our feet are cooled, sometimes numbed, by an ice-cold mountain stream; our bodies meld into warm sand at the beach; and a soft rain feels like a thousand wet kisses. Outdoors we can hear a symphony of natural sounds, from bees buzzing to the roar of wind, or we can bask in the incredible peace of silence.

Connecting with nature evokes a sense of awe and wonderment about the universe. We are humbled by the magnitude of a mountain range and delighted by the colors of a rainbow. At the same time, we experience a oneness with the natural world, which encourages us to appreciate and respect all life. Nature calls us to be present in the moment so that we do not miss the intricate design of a spiderweb or the flash of a hummingbird.

The more we become one with nature, the more it offers us. In the wilderness we transcend time and space; we are renewed. Hikes in the woods, bodysurfing in the ocean, and even walks around the block become moving meditations, enhancing our intuition.

Look for signs and messages in the great outdoors, the symbolism of leaves falling in your path, and the pattern of birds in flight. Or simply enjoy the bliss of connecting to the natural world.

◇ ◇ ◇

POWER IN HONESTY
STAYING TRUE TO YOUR WORD

Promises are easily made. Keeping them often proves more difficult, because when we are pressured to strive always for perfection, we find it simpler to agree to undertake impossible tasks than to say no. Likewise, there is an infinite array of circumstances that conspire to goad us into telling falsehoods, even when we hold a great reverence for truth.

When you endeavor to consistently keep your word, however, you protect your reputation and promote yourself as someone who can be trusted to be unfailingly truthful. Although your honesty may not always endear you to others — for there will always be those who fear the truth — you can nonetheless be certain that your integrity is never tarnished by the patina of deceit. Since frankness and sincerity form the basis of all life-enriching relationships, your word is one of your most precious and powerful possessions.

When we promise more than we can deliver, hide from the consequences of our actions through falsehoods, or deny our true selves to others, we hurt those who were counting on us by proving that their faith was wrongly given. We are also hurt by the lies we tell and the promises we break. Integrity is the foundation of civilization, allowing people to live, work, and play side by side without fear or apprehension.

As you cultivate honesty within yourself, you will find that your honor and reliability put people at ease. Others will feel comfortable seeking out your friendship and collaborating with you on projects of great importance, certain that their positive expectations will be met. If you do catch yourself in a lie, ask yourself what you wanted to hide and why you felt that you could not be truthful. And if life's surprises prevent you from keeping your word, simply admit your error apologetically and make amends quickly.

Since the path of truth frequently represents the more difficult journey, embarking on it builds character. You can harness the power of your word when you do your best to live a life of honesty and understand what motivates *dis*honesty. In keeping your agreements and embodying sincerity, you prove that you are worthy of trust and that you perceive values as something to be incorporated into your daily existence.

◇ ◇ ◇

A PLACE FOR WORRIES
SURRENDER BOX

There are times when our minds grow too full. Our heads may become so crowded with our to-do lists, worries, plans, and dreams that we do not have room to think. We may believe that we are somehow taking care of our desires and concerns by keeping them at the forefront of our minds. In maintaining our mental hold on every detail, however, we may actually delay the realization of our dreams and the resolution of our worries because we do not let them go. At times such as these, we may want to use a surrender box.

A surrender box allows us to let go of our concerns and desires so that the universe can take care of them for us. We write down what we want or need to happen and then place the note into a box. By doing so, we are taking action and letting the universe know that we need help and are willing to surrender our feelings. We give ourselves permission not to be concerned with a particular problem any longer and to trust that the universe is taking care of it.

You may even want to decorate your box and keep it in a special place. It is a sacred container for your worries and desires. By letting go of them and dropping them into your box, you are giving your burden over to a higher power. Once you do, you free your mind so that you can be fully present in each moment.

Surrendering our fears and concerns and placing them in the hands of the universe does not mean that we have given up or have been defeated. Instead, we are releasing the realization of our desires and the resolution of our worries and are no longer concerning ourselves with their outcomes. It is always fun to go back and pull the slips of paper out of the box once our requests have been granted. And it is amazing how quickly problems go away and dreams come true when we finally let go and allow a higher power to help us.

◇ ◇ ◇

NOURISHMENT FOR THE SOUL
BREAKING BREAD TOGETHER

As we rush to keep up with the speed of our busy lives, one of the first activities we tend to sacrifice is the sharing of a meal with other people. We may find ourselves eating alone at the kitchen counter or hurriedly drinking a cup of soup while driving in our car.

Yet taking the time to share a meal with family or a close friend not only feeds your body, but can also nourish your soul. Companionship can fill the heart the way warm stew can satisfy your belly. Eating with others allows you to slow down while nurturing your relationships.

Breaking bread with others can be treated like a ritual where the gestures of sharing and togetherness are just as important as the food you eat. Planning, preparing, and consuming a meal are all stepping-off points for good conversation, bonding, and learning about someone else.

Inviting a new acquaintance to partake in a meal can be the start of a wonderful friendship. A shared breakfast can be a brainstorming session between co-workers, or it can set the tone for a positive day for family members. Lunch with a friend can be a welcome break from daily stress, as well as a chance to unwind. Dinner with loved ones can be a chance to talk about the day's events with people who truly care. Sometimes there might not even be a need for conversation and you may want to share a meal with someone while sitting in comfortable silence.

The breaking of bread can be a fulfilling experience, especially when done among people you love and trust. So the next time you find yourself rushing through a meal in front of your computer, you may want to pause and reconsider. The warm feelings, sense of security, and enjoyment you derive from sharing a meal with others may be the kind of break you really need.

◇ ◇ ◇

MOVING ON
OUTGROWING SPACES

While some people live their whole lives in the same house they were born in, most of us move multiple times, inhabiting many different spaces in the course of our lives. Rooms, houses, and cities all have their own energy fields; and while the energy of a place may have served us beautifully at one point, it can actually be detrimental, or just uninspiring, at another.

We need different types of energy at different times in our lives. For example, we may be in great need of peace and quiet at a certain point and move into a home that helps us feel safe and protected. Once our energy is restored, however, that same place might seem stifling and restrictive. A home filled with memories can be warm and comforting for a time but may become energetically oppressive if we want to feel free of the past.

It is important that we honor any signals we receive that indicate we may have energetically outgrown our current residence. Sometimes we stay in a living situation not because it is inspiring, but because it is convenient. And yet to really thrive in our lives, we need to think *beyond* convenience. We must commit to surrounding ourselves with the energetic qualities that most support our growth and well-being.

If you are feeling as if you may have outgrown your space, take some time to evaluate why you were first drawn to it and what it has offered you. Do you want to move for the right reasons, or do you just want to run away? Honor and acknowledge the ways in which your space has helped you and the ways in which it may be holding you back. This will assist you in clarifying what you need in your next home. Once you understand the energetic qualities you want, you can begin to visualize your next dwelling place, setting the universe in motion to help you find it.

◇ ◇ ◇

A QUEST OF THE HEART
FINDING YOUR SOUL'S PURPOSE

Destiny, the greatest mystery in every individual's life, is a grand puzzle waiting to be solved. It is not uncommon to ask, "Why am I here?" or to wish for a more dynamic or creative approach to living while still following the expected path or bowing to the status quo.

However, all individuals have been blessed with talents and strengths that flow from the depths of the soul, allowing them to make a unique and special contribution to the world. This is the root of the soul's purpose, which is much more than a simple occupation. It is the longing of the heart, a gift we ache to express, and a life's mission. Many people never discover their individual soul's purpose because they believe themselves unqualified or ill equipped for it. However, finding it is not a relay of trial and error, but an exciting journey.

The world needs the fruits of your soul's purpose, but to follow the path of the heart demands patience and courage. Until that mission is found, material successes can feel empty and unfulfilling. Finding your soul's purpose is an individual quest of introspection requiring inner counsel strong enough to disregard naysayers.

Begin by asking yourself which pursuits give you, or have given you, the most joy. Which draw upon your natural talents and cause you to feel that you have put forth deep roots in the universe? If you can think of no such activity, it is time to try something new, perhaps in the form of a hobby or volunteering. When answers do come through meditation or participation, it will be necessary to accept that large-scale changes may be in order to align your path with your soul's purpose. Although doubt may arise, fulfilling your life's mission will give you strength.

There are, however, no absolutes. Achieving the soul's purpose requires not only awareness, but participation as well. The soul exists to evolve, and when you become aware of its desires, it is up to you to take the first steps, however difficult they may be. Having fulfilled one purpose, you may find that another may arise, leading you to other paths you never anticipated. Once you have discovered your soul's purpose and embarked upon the journey, though, you will have taken the most important step in creating a truly joyful life.

◇ ◇ ◇

TEACHING BALANCE
THE NEGATIVE EFFECTS OF SPOILING CHILDREN

Parents are moved by instinct to love, nurture, and provide for their offspring. Since our children are so much a part of us, we want to see them blissfully happy. Also, our own desire to be liked, materialistic pressures, and a fervent wish that our children have everything we lacked as youngsters can prompt us to spoil them.

While it might seem that buying your children expensive gifts will give them fond memories of childhood or that you can heal your emotional wounds by doting on them, you may be unconsciously interfering with their evolutionary development. One of the most precious gifts you can grant your sons and daughters is the true independence they gain when they learn to earn what they covet and become stewards of their own happiness.

Try allowing your children to experience life to the fullest. Let them work and earn what they want. When the time comes for them to go to college and enter the workforce, you will have the assurance that you have raised a child who can both enter and contribute to society confidently.

When children are not afforded the opportunity to explore self-reliance, to understand that possessions come with a price, and to fulfill their own needs, they develop a sense of entitlement that blinds them to the necessity of hard work and the needs of others. We may spoil children because giving them gifts is pleasurable. Or we may want to avoid conflict for fear that they will not love us.

Yet those who are given acceptance, caring, and affection in abundance are often kinder, more charitable, and more responsible than those whose parents accede to their every material demand. They develop a strong sense of self that stretches beyond possessions and the approval of their peers, and as adults they understand that each individual is responsible for building the life he or she desires. If you find yourself giving in to your child's every whim, ask yourself why. You may discover that you are trying to answer for what you feel is lacking in your own life.

Rearing your children to respect the value of money and self-sufficiency as they grow from infants to young adults is a challenging but rewarding process. It can be difficult to watch them struggle to meet a personal goal, yet wonderful to be by their side as they achieve it. Your choice not to spoil your children will bless you with more opportunities to show them understanding and compassion and to be fully present with them as they journey toward adulthood.

◇ ◇ ◇

BECOMING A BEACON OF LIGHT
MEDITATING OUTWARD

All humans are beings of energy, vibrating at unique and beautiful frequencies. As such, each of us possesses the ability to affect the world in a positive way simply by using focused meditation to connect with our own environments, our fellow humans, and the earth. Since it is intention that creates the connection, we all have the potential to act as beacons of light—centers of positive, healing energy that radiate outward, dispelling negativity and spreading joy and well-being. This entails more than choosing to maintain a positive attitude. Becoming a beacon of light means embodying qualities of energy that can open up the potential of others, along with being a center of positive change by meditating outward.

The process begins with creating an environment that is supportive and energizing—a sanctuary where those who enter your space can find renewal. That is the seed. To make it blossom, sit in a quiet place and begin breathing deeply, focusing on achieving a clear and calm state of mind. Center yourself and visualize a blanket of warm, positive energy flowing over your hands. When you can perceive it shifting and having an effect on the air around you, direct the energy into your body. Release it and let it spiral outward, first into your home; then into the yard or surrounding residences; then over your entire neighborhood and through your city, state, and country. Finally, let the gentle vortex of perfect light and perfect love you have created settle over the entire world. As you send out your loving thoughts, realize that you are the center and the source of the beacon.

When you have spread your gift of positive energy as far as it will travel, return your focus to the place from which it originated and take a moment to observe your own feelings. As you take one last deep breath, reflect upon the fact that in brightening your own soul, you have played a positive role in the spiritual evolution of all people. And in blessing your own home, you have also blessed the earth.

◇ ◇ ◇

FULLY COMMITTED TO NOW
WHY WE ARE NOT SHOWN THE BIG PICTURE

Sometimes we may find ourselves wishing we knew what our lives were going to look like or what gifts and challenges were going to be presented to us in the coming months or years. We may want to know if the relationship we are in now will go the distance or if our goals will be realized. Perhaps we feel as if we need help making a decision and we want to know which choice will work out best.

We may consult psychics, tarot cards, our dreams, and many other sources in the hopes of finding out what the future holds. Usually, at most, we may catch glimpses. And even though we think that we would like to know the whole story in all its details, the truth is that we would probably be overwhelmed and exhausted if we were aware of everything that is going to happen to us.

Just think of your life as you have lived it up to this point. If you are like most of us, you have probably done and faced more than you could have ever imagined. If someone had told you as a child about all the jobs and relationships you would experience, along with each one's inherent ups and downs, you would have become overwhelmed. With your head full of information about the future, you would have had a very hard time experiencing your life in the present moment, which is where everything actually happens.

In many ways, not knowing what the future has in store brings out the qualities you need to grow. For example, it would have been difficult to commit yourself to certain people or projects if you knew that they would not ultimately work out, yet it was through your dedication to seeing them through that you experienced the lessons you needed to grow. Looking back on your life, you would very likely be hard-pressed to say that anything in your past should not have happened. In fact, your most challenging experiences, with their inevitable lessons, may have ultimately brought you the greatest rewards.

Not knowing the future keeps us just where we need to be—fully committed and in the present moment.

◇ ◇ ◇

STEPPING INTO CONSCIOUSNESS
BEING AWARE

Life is a journey that comprises many steps on our personal path, taking us down a winding road of constant evolution. Each day we are provided with a myriad of opportunities that can allow us to transform into our next best selves. One moment we are presented with a chance to react differently when someone in our life rubs us the wrong way; at another, we may find ourselves wanting to walk away from a particular situation but unsure if we can.

Eventually, we may find ourselves stuck in a rut that we can never seem to get out of. We may even make the same choices over and over again because we do not know how to choose otherwise. Rather than moving us forward, our personal paths may take us in a seemingly never-ending circle where our actions and decisions lead us only to where we have already been. It is during these moments that awareness can be the first step to change.

Awareness is when we are able to realize what we are doing. We observe ourselves, noticing our actions, reactions, and choices as if we were a detached viewer. Awareness is the first step in the direction of transformation because we cannot make a change unless we are conscious that one needs to be made in the first place. We can then begin understanding why we are doing what we are doing. Afterward, it becomes difficult *not* to change, since we are no longer asleep to the truth behind our behaviors. We also begin to realize that just as we are the source of the causes of our actions, we are also the originator of any changes that we want to happen.

Freedom comes with awareness. Rather than thinking we are stuck in a repetitive cycle where there is no escape, we begin to see that we very much play a hand in creating our lives. Whether we are mindful of them or not, our choices are always ours to make. Our past and our present no longer have to dictate our future when we choose to be aware. We are then free to move beyond our old limits, make different choices, and take new actions. Our paths cannot help but wind us forward in our lives while paving the way for novel experiences and ways of being. It is through awareness that we can continue to consciously evolve.

◇ ◇ ◇

FORGIVING YOURSELF
RELEASING GUILT

We all know what it is like to feel guilty about something, and many of us struggle with this feeling all the time. Guilt makes us feel that we are somehow unforgivable. While this experience is common, it is detrimental to our overall well-being. Feeling guilty generally promotes a sense of powerlessness — an anguished agonizing over a past action that cannot be changed. The problem with this is that it does not inspire us to forgive ourselves, make amends, and move forward free of emotions that no longer serve us.

Originally, *guilt* referred to the fine paid for proven wrongdoing. Once you made the payment, in time or money, for what you had done, you were free of the sentence and the guilt. The problem with guilt as it is often experienced now is that it becomes a permanent state of mind for some people. In this case, it is a neurotic preoccupation rather than a fair assessment of misconduct followed by a course of action that leads to reparation.

It is part of the human experience to make choices and hurt others. There is no way to avoid this entirely, and wallowing in guilt will not help you or anyone else, nor will it prevent future suffering. Understanding this is the first step toward liberating yourself from this negative emotion.

If you are hanging on to guilt about something, the first thing you need to do is practice compassion for yourself—you are human and you make choices. Compassion and self-forgiveness are much more effective in helping you determine a course of effective action than guilt. You may need to offer an apology, or you might have to make some changes in yourself. Know that with each action, you create healing for yourself and anyone you have hurt. Finally, learn from your choices, but never beat yourself up. Know that you are inherently good, love yourself, and always do your best . . . then there will be no place for guilt in your life.

◇ ◇ ◇

DIFFERENT WAYS OF NAVIGATING
WE ARE ALL IN THE SAME BOAT

We are all in the same boat. We just have different paddles, and perhaps we find ourselves on different rivers. We
all live in human bodies — these are the vehicles in which
we move through our world. We are all made of flesh,
blood, and bone, with brains, hearts, and lungs to power us.
Our paddles (that is, the tools we use to move through the
world) vary, as do the bodies of water (the environments) in
which we find ourselves.

Some of us harness our high IQs to get where we want
to go. Some of us use our smiles; others employ kindness, a
gift with language, or athletic ability. Many of these qualities
we were born with, and others are skills we have learned.

Considering this metaphor in relation to your own life
can be very enlightening. What tools are you using to get
from point A to point B on your journey? Chances are, you
and the people you know have used many different tools in

various combinations throughout your lives to get where you needed to go. Just as with oars or paddles, a balanced approach is best. If you rely too much on one thing, such as beauty, to open doors, you fail to be well rounded and may eventually fail to maintain your equilibrium. And if you lose that one quality, you have no paddle at all. This is inspiration to develop multiple tools to navigate your world.

Some of us may be moving along paths that are like rushing rivers; others may be on a large, still lake. We have all felt, at one time or another, tossed about on a stormy ocean. Through all of this, we are never really alone, even though it might seem so. There is inspiration everywhere around us in the form of other people making their way in the world in the very same boat.

Remember to look around you for role models, companionship, and encouragement.

◇ ◇ ◇

ANATOMY OF A FLOWER
BEING PART OF THE WHOLE

As with every living thing, a flower's intention is pro-creation. All its various parts work together toward this purpose, and each plays an essential role in the process. The vivid, delicate blooms attract pollinators (birds and bees) who aid in the transfer of pollen. The center is the source and inspiration for the visually stunning petals — which, in turn, attract what the flower needs to create seeds and multiply.

When you have an opportunity to serve something larger than your individual self, you are like a petal on a flower, offering your particular brand of beauty and charisma in the service of a centralizing force: a person with a higher vision, a community with a common goal, or a spiritual path. Contemplate the ways in which you are a petal on the flower of your life. Who or what is at the center? What core values are you serving?

Consider, too, any situations in which you are the center of the flower, offering the nourishing seeds of an idea or quality that others are willing to gather around and perpetuate. It takes confidence and vision to be the nucleus. It also requires humility to empower the "petals" around you that are helping feed your vision and enabling it to grow beyond you.

Like the parts of a flower, we are all here working together to create and be creative. Whether we are the center or the petal, it helps to be conscious of the seeds we are sowing in the world, as this is how we forge the future.

In essence, we are all petals radiating outward from the unified source of energy that is life. Our time on this earthly plane is finite and fragile, yet we branch out from our invisible source vibrantly and powerfully, attracting energy and making fertile connections that contribute to the continuation of life itself.

◇ ◇ ◇

THINKING SMALL
LIFE'S LITTLE VICTORIES

Many of us are taught from an early age to strive for big dreams and seek out equally large successes. We find inspiration in those who have overcome the greatest odds and who have built the largest empires. We seldom look to our own lives for examples of victories, forgetting that any accomplishment deserves a moment of triumph. Life's little achievements encompass both the moments that make you give an inner shout of joy and simple things such as a job well done, finishing a daunting task, or making it through a less-than-pleasant situation.

Little victories can keep you optimistic about the big ones and help you retain a positive attitude even when things are going wrong, because the small successes will stick with you if you take time to honor them. Look carefully . . . you will no doubt find them occurring throughout your day. Did you keep your cool in a tense situation? Resist the urge to spend unwisely? Find time to spend with your family? Pat yourself on the back when you notice a small success and make a mental note of it, or write down a few things each day that can be considered little victories. Make your accounts detailed by outlining exactly what caused you to feel triumphant.

When you choose not to acknowledge life's little victories, deeming them insignificant, it is easy to become frustrated. Instead of staking your happiness on getting a promotion, buying a new car, or being the winner, stake it on your ability to conquer the ups and downs and responsibilities inherent in living. In doing so, you will find yourself able to avoid being caught up in negative feelings by keeping one eye toward your next triumph.

◇ ◇ ◇

LESSONS OF DISCOVERY
INSTRUCTION MANUALS FOR LIVING

Depending on what stage we are at in our lives, we can sometimes feel as if we ought to know more about who we are or how to live. We may even berate ourselves for making the same choices or for just not "getting it," whatever "it" may be. We wonder how our lives would be now if only we had "known better." During moments such as these, it is important to remember that none of us comes into the world with an instruction manual and that learning lessons is a lifelong journey.

Inherent in our being born is the fact that we are here to observe, learn, and grow. Accompanying this is a built-in guarantee that there will be misadventures along the way. And while it is only natural that we may sometimes become overwhelmed, especially when the lessons keep coming, it is important to remember that learning to understand ourselves and our world is an ongoing and active process where the journey is more important than the destination.

The intent of every lesson is for you to become more of who you are. And as you grow through this self-discovery, you begin to create your *own* instruction manual. The hows and whys are yours to discover, and part of the beauty of being alive is that these rules are always changing.

If you feel that you would like to explore what your personal instruction manual may already say, then try writing down some of the significant events in your life in the order that they have happened to you. It is also important to take note of what insight you gained from each one. When you are done, you may be surprised to discover how much you are always growing and that every lesson learned informs the one that comes next.

That said, there is never any need to be hard on yourself or to think that you should have it all figured out. You always know as much as you are meant to know at any given moment, and growing into your fullness is a process that unfolds with divine timing. You and your life are beautiful works in progress. Discover yourself and embrace your life's lessons and your instruction manual will create itself.

◇ ◇ ◇

WAITING FOR THE OTHER SHOE TO DROP
FOCUSING ON NEGATIVE POSSIBILITIES

Many people who find themselves in a positive situation look around suspiciously for the catch. Or they unconsciously brace themselves for the bad that they believe must necessarily follow the good. It is easy to think that favorable fortune is too good to last and that happiness is always fleeting, but waiting for the other shoe to drop or for the rug to be pulled out from under your feet is not healthy. Always focusing on the negative possibilities can put you on edge and even *invite* those possibilities.

While you remain hypervigilant, you necessarily must wait, doing your best to protect yourself from uncertain events. It becomes more difficult to enjoy happiness and success when you are on guard against what will come next. There are, however, steps that you can take to address this tendency by confronting your feelings and discovering what is standing in the way of optimism.

The fear that happiness is temporary is often rooted in the subconscious mind and past experiences that have fostered a pessimistic outlook. We are often afraid to trust in our own potential or we feel guilty when our lives go too well because we do not believe we deserve success. The truth is that we *do,* and there is no reason that a boon must be followed by a loss.

When you find yourself waiting for the other shoe to drop, ask yourself if there is a strong possibility that something negative will happen, or if your mind has conjured up the fear that your positive situation cannot last. If your subconscious is telling you that you do not deserve happiness, counter it by reaffirming your worth. Put a motivational affirmation on display in your home or office, or create a positive mantra—then focus on the present. The future is unknown, so give yourself permission to enjoy the things going well for you right now.

It may take time for you to fully believe that you have control over your own happiness and that you can hold on to that contentment without worrying about what the future will bring. You may want to remember that you have more power over your life than you realize. The other shoe may or may not drop, but it is your own attitude that will ultimately let you hold on to the result of good things in life while letting go of the bad.

◇ ◇ ◇

BEINGS OF LIGHT
HUMAN ANGELS

During each of our journeys, there are those inevitable moments when someone comes into our life at precisely the right time and says or does precisely the right thing. Their words or actions may help us perceive ourselves more clearly, remind us that everything will turn out for the best, help us cope, or see us through difficult situations. These people are human angels—individuals designated by the universe to be of service to those in need at specific points in time. Some human angels make a commitment before birth to make a positive contribution to the world at a particular moment. Others were chosen by the universe. All, however, come into our lives when we least expect them and when we can most benefit from their presence.

A few of the human angels we may encounter are in professions where helping others is an everyday occurrence, but most of them are regular people, going about their daily lives until called upon to be in the right place at the right time to bring peace, joy, and help or to heal some-one when they most need it. You may have met a human angel in the form of a teacher who gave you a piece of advice that touched your soul and influenced your path. The person who momentarily stopped you to say hello on the street, delaying you long enough to avoid an oncom-ing car, is also a human angel. This individual may offer nothing more than a kind word or a smile, but will do so when you can draw the most strength and support from this simple action.

You may be a human angel and not know it. Your fate or intuition may guide you toward other people's challeng-ing or distressing situations, leading you to infer that you simply have bad luck. But recognizing yourself as a human angel can help you deal with the pain you see and under-stand that you are there to help and comfort others during their times of need.

Human angels give their inner light to all who need it, coming into our lives and often changing us forever. Their task has its challenges, but they have the power to teach, bring us joy, and comfort us during moments of despair.

◇ ◇ ◇

HEIGHTS OF AWARENESS
HIGHLY SENSITIVE PEOPLE

Some people are born into the world with their ears and eyes open to the strong energy pulsating all around them. They experience everyday sensory input in a uniquely heightened way that can cause both pleasure and pain. In an environment overflowing with subtleties of thought, as well as chemicals, noise, light, scents, and both positive and negative energy, these highly sensitive people do not have the ability to filter the emotions, substances, and sensations they take in. They can be easily overwhelmed in crowds and may require quiet time alone to regroup their feelings. But highly sensitive people are far from being weak. On the contrary, they are strong, perceptive, intuitive, and exceptionally artistic individuals who have a wonderful gift of insight to offer.

Highly sensitive people feel emotions deeply and, since they tend to be empathic, find themselves affected by the emotions of others, even those of actors or characters in books. Because of this, they are perceptive of people's needs, joys, and pains; and they cannot simply dismiss their feelings. They are as hurt by an insult to another as they would be by one directed at them and try to avoid most conflict. When faced with negative emotions or situations, highly sensitive people can easily suffer from depression or anxiety. Their unique mode of perception allows them to develop a strong appreciation for nature, music, art, and literature. Many talented artists are sensitive, and most sensitive people are artistic in some way.

This sensitivity exerts itself physically as well, which can cause the nervous system to become overloaded when faced with bright lights, loud noises, strong tastes, or erratic environments. Such people may be allergic to a number of foods, fabrics, and chemicals. Thus, they fare best in peaceful, harmonious settings that offer strong support, and may find that they build their strongest bonds with other highly sensitive people who understand their needs. To minimize stress, it can be beneficial to create a daily routine, seek out calming activities, avoid jarring noise and lighting, meditate, and use relaxing essential oils.

Although some highly sensitive people develop animosity toward their way of experiencing the world, it should be understood that it is not a curse, but a path to wisdom. Denying your sensitivity can lead to unhappiness, but exploring its benefits can bring about positive change in yourself and others, particularly when you choose to seek out the world's beauty and demonstrate to others the heights it can reach.

◇ ◇ ◇

OVERCOMING OBSTACLES
NOTHING IS INSURMOUNTABLE

When our next best course of action seems unclear, any dilemmas we face can appear insurmountable. Yet there is nothing we cannot overcome with time, persistence, focused thought, help, and faith. Whatever the situation or problem, there is always a solution.

If you remember to look within, even as you search around you for the right course of action, you will always be able to center yourself, clear your mind, and see that nothing has to be impossible. The first step in overcoming an obstacle is to *believe* that it can be overcome. Doing so will give you the strength and courage to move through any crisis. The second step is to make a resolution that you can prevail over any chaos.

Enlist your support network of family and friends if necessary. The more minds there are to consider a problem, the more solutions can be found. Do not discount ideas just because they seem impractical or unrealistic, and do not keep searching for the perfect alternative. Often there is no "best" choice; there is only the one you make so that you can begin moving beyond whatever is obstructing our path. At the very least coming to a decision, even if is not the ideal one, can give you a sense of peace before you have to figure out what your next course of action will be.

If you feel overwhelmed by the scope of your troubles, you may want to think of other people who have turned adversity into triumph. We often gain a fresh perspective when we remember others who have overcome larger obstacles. It can be inspiring to hear of their victories, helping us remember that there is always light at the end of every tunnel. It is during our darkest hours that we sometimes need to remind ourselves that we do not have to feel helpless.

You have within and around you the resources to find a solution to any problem. And remember that if a choice you make does not work, you are always free to try another. Believe that you can get through anything and you will always prevail.

◇ ◇ ◇

A LIBERATING GOOD-BYE

CUTTING CORDS

In every relationship, people are constantly exchanging energy that can become a cord connecting two individuals. This energetic link forms just below the breastbone and can remain long after a relationship has ended. Such an unbroken cord may leave an open channel between you and another person, through which emotions and energy can continue to flow.

If you are unaware that the cord exists, it is easy to feel the other person's emotions and mistakenly think that they are yours. Besides the fact that this can limit the amount of closure you experience in a relationship, letting this tie remain intact can leave you with a continued sense of sadness while creating feelings of lethargy as your own energy is sapped from you. Cutting the cord can help you separate yourself from old baggage and unnecessary attachments, releasing you from connections that are no longer serving you.

Finding and severing unwanted cords is a simple, gentle process that is best done alone and when you are relaxed. It is important that you be strong in your intention to release the cord between you and someone else.

To begin, breathe deeply and perform a simple centering meditation. When you are ready, visualize or sense the cords that are connecting you to other people. Run your fingers through them to separate them until you find the one you wish to cut. There is no need to worry, because the cord you need to sever will feel just right. When you have found it, determine where the cut should be made and then visualize the cord being cleanly sliced through. If you need assistance, the archangel Michael can be called upon to help you with his sword. Afterward, if you feel that cutting the cord has left spaces in your energy field, visualize them being filled with healing sunlight.

There may be times when cutting a cord can help free a relative or loved one to reach new stages of growth. You are not severing a relationship, but rather the cords that are no longer benefiting either of you. At other times, a cord may simply refuse to be cut because it is still serving a higher purpose. It is also important to remember that cutting a cord with someone is not a replacement for doing your emotional work with him or her. It can, however, be an enactment of that work upon its completion. In any case, severing a relationship cord should always be viewed as a positive and nurturing act. By cutting those that no longer need to be there, you are setting yourself and others free from the ties that bind.

◇ ◇ ◇

A CYCLE OF POWER
HONORING MENSTRUATION

In the ancient past as humanity began to move toward a patriarchal society, women were gradually deprived of the awareness of a wonderful gift. Previously, menstruation was considered a miraculous and cosmic event in which women were strongly connected to all things spiritual. A menstruating female was thought to be at the height of her power and was encouraged to spend time looking inward for feminine wisdom. Her menses held *mana*, or the "breath of life," and was a source of nourishment for the fertile soil.

As the goddesses were cast aside, so, too, was women's relationship with the lunar cycles and the tides. Those menstruating were forced to remain apart lest they infect others with their uncleanliness, and their wisdom was suppressed. Contradicting today's attitudes of shame, however, is a strong movement seeking to reclaim the power of menstruation and see it as a supreme blessing rather than a curse.

For many women, menstruation is a time of altered awareness, creativity, spirituality, and new heights of intuition. The need for solitude or rest is unjustly perceived as a weakness; in reality, it indicates a strong urge for introspection during the menstrual cycle. Perception and sensitivity are both amplified, encouraging women to challenge themselves and others. The Native American tradition states that a menstruating woman has the potential to be more spiritually powerful than any male or female at any time.

Some may experience these changes during different spans of the cycle. It is not uncommon to experience a stillness and desire for quiet during the first part of the menses and extreme clarity during the latter part. In ignoring or denying such feelings, men and women alike lose touch with feminine power and the awareness of the value of menstruation.

It may be helpful to understand that this is a natural time within the moon cycle to retreat from worldly concerns and embrace transformation. Women may enter into the cycle one way and find that they emerge renewed on the other side. Harnessing the inherent power means listening to intuition, noticing unique synchronicities, and understanding the core of oneself. It is a gift from the body to the earth and from the body to the mind.

◇ ◇ ◇

SEASONS OF BEAUTY
AGING GRACEFULLY

We tend to associate youth with beauty, but the truth is that beauty transcends every age. Just as a deciduous tree is stunning in all its stages — from its full leafy-green appearance in the summer to its naked skeleton during winter and everything in between — human beings are beautiful throughout their life spans.

Our early years tend to be about learning and experiencing as much as we possibly can. We move through the world like sponges, absorbing the ideas of other people and our surroundings. Like a tree in spring, we are waking up to the universe. In this youthful phase of life, our physical strength, freshness, and beauty help open doors and attract attention.

Gradually, we begin to use the information we have gathered to form ideas and opinions of our own. As we cultivate our philosophy about life, our beauty becomes as much about what we are saying, doing, and creating as it is about our appearance. Like a tree in summer, we become full, expressive, gorgeous, and productive.

When the time comes for us to let go of the creations of our middle lives, we are like a tree in autumn dropping leaves as we release our past attachments and prepare for a new phase of growth. The children move on, and careers shift or end. The lines on our faces, the stretch marks, and the gray hairs are beautiful testaments to the fullness of our experience.

In the winter of our lives, we become stripped down to our essence like a tree. We may grow more radiant than ever at this stage, because our inner light shines more brightly through our eyes as time passes. Attractiveness at this age originates in the very core of our being—our essence. This essence is a reminder that there is nothing to fear in growing older and that there is a kind of beauty that comes only after one has spent many years on Earth.

◇ ◇ ◇

HONORING LIFE CHANGES
BLESSINGWAY

A Mother Blessing is a ritual adapted from the traditional Navajo ceremony known as a Blessingway to fill a gap in Western celebrations surrounding birth. Whereas a baby shower celebrates the coming of the child, a Mother Blessing commemorates the woman's passage into motherhood. Friends — generally all female, but not always — gather to give her their support as she approaches one of the most intense experiences of her life. A Father Blessing is also a wonderful idea, especially during a time when fathers may feel a little left out.

A Blessingway ceremony can be given in honor of anyone going through a major life transition. From graduating high school to turning 50, significant life changes deserve to be acknowledged and celebrated. Many of our traditional ways of recognizing these transitions have become hollow, often dominated by consumerism. A Blessingway is less about giving gifts and more about communicating from the heart, offering words of encouragement and inspiration to buoy the guest of honor in the face of major change.

Often at Mother Blessings each participant brings a bead to give to the mother, and a necklace or bracelet is made for her. Each person presents her with the bead and says something that is wished for on her journey — strength, courage, or a sense of humor, for example. People can also give their bead in honor of a quality she already has that they believe will make her a good mother. This way she leaves the ritual with a magical talisman imbued with the loving energy of her community. She can carry this into labor or hang it over her baby's crib as a reminder of the strength she harbors within and the love surrounding her. The same idea can be adapted to fit Blessingways in honor of retirement, a new job, a major move, or even a divorce.

If someone you know is approaching a momentous rite of passage, organize a Blessingway in the person's honor. Or, if *you* need one, ask for it. You could create a beautiful new tradition in your community of friends and family.

◇ ◇ ◇

HAWK MEDICINE
THE POWER OF PERSPECTIVE

Hawks have the power to soar high above the earth, giving them a perspective previously only available to the inhabitants of the celestial sphere above. Because of this, people from various cultures throughout history have seen them as messengers of spirit, bringing wisdom from the heavens and the value of their higher vision down to Earth.

From their vantage point, riding on the wind and bathed in sunlight, they remind us today that there is a bigger picture to be seen. When we get bogged down with the details of what is right in front of us, hawks help us remember that we are part of a larger plan and that everything fits together beautifully and perfectly. Once in this expanded frame of mind, we can harness their reputation as visionaries, using their keen eyesight to focus on the exact spot that truly needs our attention. Hawks teach us how to interpret and then follow our personal vision through inspiration and focus on our goal.

These birds of prey were thought to be able to stare directly into the sun and see what is not visible to the rest of us. Using our spiritual vision, we, too, can look deeply into the inner light that guides us, seeing clearly what is not perceptible unless sought: our personal truth glowing within us. With that knowledge, we, like the hawk, can confidently ride the winds of chance, moving as one with the flow of whirling energy. This ability is what inspired the Egyptians to make hawks the hieroglyphic symbol for the wind.

The ability of hawks to live on land but visit the sky is a good reminder for us all. Their strength and survival comes from communing regularly with the spirit and bringing the guidance received into earthly affairs. Soaring in the province of the heavenly bodies—among the sun, the stars, and the wind that moves the clouds—reminds us to consider a larger perspective, one that inspires us to travel through the world we inhabit with strength, certainty, and grace.

◇ ◇ ◇

PEELING THE ONION
BREAKING THROUGH BARRIERS

The human psyche is almost infinitely complex, made up of layers upon layers of thoughts, experiences, emotions, fears, loves, and goals. Those who seek to find the true essence of being or move past a fear find that there are many intermediate steps along the way. As we first look inward, we view ourselves as a whole when in fact we are only seeing the surface. Like an onion, if we move past the surface, we will find another layer, and beyond that we find another.

These layers are barriers, and everyone has them. You may work past one fear, only to be confronted with a deeper, underlying fear. Or you may fully assimilate a revelation, only to find other aspects of it that you had not discovered. How many layers you will confront before encountering a resolution is unknown. This is the journey — this is life.

But the journey to the center of the onion — what is called *sunyata* in Sanskrit or *mu* in Chinese — can be an enlightening experience in and of itself. As you break through each barrier, you will gain a more profound understanding of your own mind and come to learn the unique facets that make up who you are. You will become intimately acquainted with your needs and wants, reactions, aversions, pleasures, and pains. You will discover qualities within yourself that have been buried by the years or by old hurts.

This knowledge is cumulative. As you break through one barrier and confront the next — oftentimes more powerful — barrier, you will be equipped with the knowledge of self that you have gained in your searching.

During the "peeling of the onion," you may feel frustrated because it can seem as if progress is slow or nonexistent. But do not let the multitude of layers bother you. Many of the qualities that make you who you are may be hidden at first. The process can continue indefinitely, for with self-discovery comes growth and thus further discovery. The more you learn, the more you will inevitably find as you travel deeper and deeper within your soul.

◇ ◇ ◇

THE WORLD IN
A BRIGHT LIGHT
GRATITUDE

Every day is a blessing, and in each moment there are many things that we can be grateful for. The world opens up to us when we live in a space of gratitude. In essence, gratitude has a snowball effect. When we are appreciative and express it, the universe glows a bit more brightly and showers us with even more blessings.

There is always something to be grateful for, even when life seems hard. When times are tough, whether we are having a bad day or are stuck in what feels like an endless rut, it may be difficult to take the time to feel grateful. Yet that is when gratitude can be most important. If we can look at our lives during periods of challenge and discover something to be thankful for, then we can transform our realities in an instant. There are blessings to be found everywhere, but when we are focusing on what is negative, our abundance can be easy to miss. Instead choosing to find things we can appreciate that already exist in our lives changes what we see in our world. We start to notice one blessing, then another.

When we constantly choose to be grateful, we see that every breath is a miracle, and each smile becomes a gift. We begin to understand that difficulties are also invaluable lessons. The sun is always shining for us when we are full of thanks, even if it is hidden behind clouds on a rainy day. A simple sandwich becomes a feast, and a trinket is transformed into a treasure.

Living in a state of appreciation allows us to spread our abundance, because that is the energy we emanate from our beings. Since the world reflects back to us what we embody, the additional bounty that inevitably flows our way gives us even more to be grateful for. The universe wants to shower us with blessings. The more we appreciate life, the more life appreciates *us* and bestows us with greater goodness.

◇ ◇ ◇

MAKING CHANGE
TRYING SOMETHING NEW EVERY DAY

Change is good. It invites us to grow, encourages us to experience new things and welcome new people into our lives, and ultimately frees us from the mundane.

Many people are not comfortable with change, preferring that every day be much like every other. There are even some who may be miserable yet reluctant to change. And a few are actually *afraid* of change.

Still, regardless of whether we like it or not, change happens. As Buddha said, "Change is the only constant." So if it is coming whether we are ready or not, it behooves us to accept it—even embrace it. Changing our relationship with "change" can greatly enhance our lives, opening up new possibilities and challenging us to become more open-minded, interesting, and positive people.

To begin accepting and welcoming change in your life, start by expanding your comfort zone and making small adjustments. Here are some ideas to help you get started:

- Take a new route to work or school, perhaps even a new mode of transportation; ride the bus, carpool, bike, or even walk if possible.

- Eat new foods. You could try something different every day—ethnic dishes, a fruit you have never tasted, or a new drink.

- Every day make an effort to talk to somebody you don't know, even if only to say hello.

- Rearrange the furniture.

- Take a class in something you know nothing about—for example, Latin American studies, Butoh, or bookbinding.

- Try a new hairstyle. Curl or straighten your hair, or change your part.

- Watch no TV for a day.

- If you drink coffee every morning, try tea, cocoa, juice, or hot water.

- Shop at a different grocery store.

- If you always shower, take a bath—or vice versa.

By taking baby steps in creating change in your life, you have chosen to act, thereby declaring to the universe that you are ready for the unfamiliar. What changes will you make today?

FINDING SIMPLE SOLUTIONS
SIMPLICITY CIRCLES

Few people would give up the chance to have more free time, be less rushed, and forge a connection with the earth, but the path to these ends seems complicated. Society equates success with money, prestige, and the accumulation of things. Throughout the world, however, people are questioning this definition of success. They are looking for ways to save time and money, to live on less, to support nature, and to feel as if they play a vital part in the universe.

People are attracted to the voluntary-simplicity movement because they want a new way to look at life, but they do not want to do it alone. A means of finding friendship, support, inspiration, intellectual stimulation, and personal transformation—simplicity circles bring together those individuals who want to discover the "good life."

A simplicity circle is a unique form of conscious learning that helps people reject excess consumerism, competitiveness, and commercialism in favor of creativity, harmony with the earth, and community. As participants discuss voluntary simplicity, they analyze their experiences and those of others. This allows them to make informed choices about what to purchase, how and where to work, how to slow down, and how to enjoy life.

But participating in a simplicity circle is more than a learning experience, and the discussions often go beyond the primary topic of rejecting the consumer culture. These gatherings are a form of gratification in which you are recognized and accepted for your heart and soul rather than for the image of success put forth by society.

Those who participate in simplicity circles have diverse reasons for doing so. Some are searching for meaning in their lives. Others question the way humanity treats the earth. Many are seeking like-minded people who have chosen the same lifestyle. The ultimate goal of each simplicity circle is to understand that all life is interdependent. Joining one can be a powerful motivator, helping you find the means to live in harmony with yourself, with others, and with Mother Earth.

◊ ◊ ◊

UNHINDERED MOVEMENT
GETTING OUT OF YOUR OWN WAY

When we find ourselves facing obstacles that appear to be blocking us from our goals, it is important to try not to get discouraged. It can be easy to feel stuck or that life is creating circumstances preventing us from getting what we want. And while it is easy to look to everyone and every-thing outside of us for the problem — perhaps even wanting to "get rid" of the person, object, or circumstance we may feel is blocking us — sometimes the best course of action to take may be to look inside *ourselves* first.

It is amazing how often we can get in our own way without even being aware that we are doing so. Even though we truly want to succeed, there are many reasons why we may sometimes block our own efforts. It could be that we are afraid to succeed, so we subconsciously create circumstances to keep ourselves stuck. Or it may be that we block ourselves by making the achievement of our goals more difficult than they really are. We might even approach our goals in a way that keeps creating the same unsuccessful results.

If you believe that you have been standing in your own way, you may want to take a piece of paper and record how you have done so. Write down the choices you have made that have hindered your efforts and the fears that may have prompted you to make these decisions. Take note of any thoughts and feelings that arise. It is important to be gentle and compassionate during this process. Try not to blame yourself for getting in your own way. Remember the choices you make always are there to serve you until it is time to let them go.

When you are finished, throw the paper away while setting an intention that you are getting rid of any obstacles you have created. You can then let yourself start again with a clean slate. Doubts and fears are going to be natural, but with this new awareness, you should be able to prevent yourself from subconsciously creating stumbling blocks. Besides, now that you have decided to get out of your own way, the part of you that has always wanted to succeed can do so.

◇ ◇ ◇

RECEIVING WITH GRACE
ACCEPTING COMPLIMENTS

Many of us find it difficult to take compliments but easy to believe the slightest criticism. Today, right now, let us make a choice to fully accept admiring remarks as we would a gift. Sincere compliments *are* gifts of praise, kudos given for wise choices or accomplishments or perhaps for just letting our light shine. There is no reason not to acknowledge the gift of kind words, but some of us argue against them, even providing reasons why they are not true.

If we visualize the energy of a compliment, we would see beautiful, shining, positive light being sent from the giver—which, if accepted graciously, would brighten our personal energy field. Our gratitude then returns to the sender as a warm, fuzzy glow, completing an even circuit of good feelings. But if we reject a compliment, what could have been a beautiful exchange becomes awkward and uncomfortable, making it a negative experience instead.

Misplaced modesty can ruin the joy of sharing this connection with another person, but we can accept admiration and still be humble by simply saying "Thank you."

However, if you reject compliments due to a lack of self-esteem, then the first step would be to start believing good things about yourself. Try giving yourself praise in the mirror. Beyond the initial feelings of silliness, you will notice how good this feels and can watch the smile it puts on your face. The next step would be to see what it is like to give compliments to others. Notice how great you feel when you have made another person's face brighten and how different your response when the gift you have offered is rejected. Having experienced all sides, you will be ready to play along fully and willingly.

We are our own harshest critics. When we accept compliments, we are reminded that others see us through different eyes. All living beings crave positive attention, and we all deserve to have uplifting energy shared with us. Perhaps if we happily and gratefully accept compliments, we will give others permission to do so as well.

◇ ◇ ◇

FEMININE WISDOM
MAIDEN, MOTHER, CRONE

A woman's life is filled with stages, milestones usher-
ing in wondrous experiential apexes such as the coming of
fertility, motherhood, and wisdom. Three aspects — *maiden,
mother,* and *crone* — have traditionally represented the boun-
ties and new beginnings represented by each stage:

- The **maiden** is the aspect of new beginnings,
  youth, playfulness, spontaneity, and learning.

- A woman in the prime of her life can be said to
  be living under the aspect of the **mother,** who
  personifies fertility, strength, and stability. She is
  the gentle nurturer as well as the fierce lioness.

- Last, and by far the most misunderstood — yet
  in many ways the most deserving of reverence
  — is the **crone,** who holds within her all the
  wisdom of the journeys of womanhood.

The word *crone* once meant "wise woman" and, in antiquity, was a term of respect. The crone was a voice of wisdom, an elder, a healer, a counselor, and a teacher who had traveled the paths of maiden and mother and possessed the accumulated insight of youth, adulthood, and old age. She represented the fulfillment of maturity and the knowledge that could only be obtained through a life well lived. The transition to cronehood was a rich and empowering experience and an important rite of passage, although not one associated with a specific age.

Even though it seems that eternal youth is an obsession today, women are now reclaiming the status once connected with cronehood by recognizing their evolution and acting upon it. In awakening the crone as she once was, women are acknowledging the extraordinary wisdom, grace, dignity, and beauty that come with maturity.

In embracing the aspect of the crone, you should be aware of the fact that age, experience, knowledge, and power are profound gifts that can never be taken from you. Every stage in life is yours and yours alone and should be embraced as a vital part of life's journey. As you pass lovingly through each one, coming finally to the remarkable crone, you will gradually be awakened to its mysteries until you hold within you the keys to them all.

◇ ◇ ◇

TIME TO INTEGRATE
SPIRITUAL PLATEAUS

It is a natural part of spiritual development to have periods of activity and growth followed by periods of relative quiet. Sometimes we need to rest in order to integrate a new vision of the world, or ourselves, taking time to assimilate realizations and let old patterns and habits fall away. The purpose of times such as these is to stabilize our new growth. While it may appear that nothing is happening, these can be necessary periods of rest and integration.

Sometimes, though, slow growth or *no* growth can actually be stagnation. We may have become attached to keeping things as they are, afraid to invite more change. Yet change is the nature of reality, and when we resist it, we fall out of sync with what is. Just as a plateau is a good location to get our bearings, to see where we have come from and where we might go next, it is also a place we must not be afraid to leave if we are to move to the next level.

There is a Zen expression: "Practice as if your hair were on fire." What this is meant to inspire is the sense that there is no good time not to be on your spiritual path. This is not to say that you cannot ever rest or stop. It is not about overachieving or overworking yourself; it is just about challenging yourself to always be awake in your life, to keep showing up in the moment. If you need to rest, do so for the present. But if you are stagnating — numbing out, escaping, or being unconscious — it is up to you to acknowledge it.

Often, stagnation settles in just before an important breakthrough. It may be a symptom of fear: one last wall thrown up by your small self in order to protect you from a life-changing realization. Sometimes it helps to explore the stagnation in order to move beyond it. Have compassion for yourself as you work to remove the obstacles to your progress. With persistence, you will be on your way to the next plateau.

◇ ◇ ◇

WARNING SIGNS
PAYING ATTENTION TO RED FLAGS

Just as the universe wants to provide for our needs, it also seeks to protect us from dangerous situations, destructive relationships, and even minor inconveniences. Frequently in our lives, perhaps every day, we encounter psychic red flags warning us of potential problems or accidents. We may not always recognize the signs; however, more often than not, we choose to ignore our intuition when it tells us that something is not right.

Red flags often come in the form of feelings urging us to pause for a moment, listen to our inner wisdom, and reconsider. We may even experience a "bad" feeling in our belly—this is a red flag letting us know that there may be a problem. We might not even be sure what the warning is about. All we know is that the universe is trying to wave us in a different direction, so we just have to pay attention and go another way.

We may even wonder whether we are paranoid or imagining things. However, when we look back at a situation or relationship where there were red flags, it becomes easy to understand exactly what those signs meant. More often than not, a red flag is not a false warning. Rather, it is the universe's way of informing us, through our own innate guidance system, that our best path lies elsewhere.

We may try to ignore the red flags waving, dismissing our unease as illogical. Yet it is always in our best interest to pay attention to them. For example, we may meet people who outwardly seem perfect. They are intelligent, attractive, and charming—although for some reason, being around them makes us uneasy. Any interactions we have with them are awkward and leave us feeling as though there were something off about the situation. These are not necessarily bad people, but for whatever reason the universe is directing us away from them.

Red flags carry your best interests at heart. No harm can ever come from stopping long enough to heed one. Pay attention to any that pop up . . . the universe is always looking out for you.

◇ ◇ ◇

KEEPING OUR MINDS SUPPLE
QUESTIONING EVERYTHING

A lot of people feel threatened if they sense that they are being asked to question their cherished beliefs or their perception of reality. Yet questioning is what keeps our minds supple and strong. Simply settling on one way of seeing things and refusing to be open to other possibilities makes us mentally rigid and generally creates a restrictive and uncomfortable atmosphere. We all know someone who refuses to budge on one or more issues, and we may have our own sacred cows that could use a little prodding. Being open-minded means that we are willing to challenge everything, including those things we take for granted.

A willingness to question even what we are sure we are right about can shake us out of complacency and reinvigorate our minds, opening us up to understanding people and perspectives that were alien to us before. This alone is good reason to remain inquisitive, no matter how much experience we have or how old we get. In the Zen tradition, this openness is known as *beginner's mind,* and it has a way of generating possibilities we could not have seen from the point of view of knowing something with certainty.

The willingness to question everything does not necessarily imply that we do not believe in anything at all, and it does not mean we have to call into doubt every single thing in the world every minute of the day. It just signals that we are humble enough to acknowledge how little we actually know about the mysterious universe we call home.

Nearly every revolutionary change in the history of human progress came about because someone questioned some time-honored belief or tradition and in doing so revealed a fresh truth, an untried way of doing things, or a new standard for ethical and moral behavior. Just so, a commitment to staying open and inquisitive in our own individual lives can lead us to new personal revolutions and truths—ones that we will hopefully, for the sake of our growth, remain open to questioning.

◇ ◇ ◇

A GROUNDING EMBRACE
HUGGING A TREE

Trees are among the world's greatest givers. Their slow and gentle life cycles provide the world with clean air, their roots filter water, and their majestically spreading branches provide shade. Full of vibrant, natural energy, trees can also give us the gifts of peace and nurturance.

Hugging or sitting with your spine against the trunk of any tree can ground your body and inspire a profound closeness with nature as the tree's energy connects to you. Making physical contact with this living thing helps you relax, alleviate stress, and sleep more deeply. Trees can absorb great amounts of energy and have the ability to soak up harmful energy from deep within you. If you are feeling anxious, sad, drained, or tense, try hugging one.

Go to the woods, a garden, or a park, and find a tree that you would like to embrace. Stand next to it and close your eyes. Relax your senses while breathing in the scent of leaves and bark. Listen to the creaking of the branches. When you feel settled, open your eyes, keeping them unfocused, and walk around the tree's trunk. Feel its unique energy as your auras meet each other.

Ask the tree for permission to touch it. If you feel it saying yes to you, begin breathing in its energy. Put your arms around the trunk and press your face to its bark. Embrace the tree for as long as you wish, feeling the roughness of its wood and the strength of its years. Relax into that strength and let it support you. You may even be able to physically feel a cyclical flow of energy taking place between your body and the tree.

If you would feel more comfortable doing so, you can sit with your back pressed to the tree for the same effect. Likewise, if you are seeking greater comfort, you may want to wrap your legs and arms around it, either at the base or by straddling a branch. Remember to thank the tree, because by hugging it, you are drinking from the well of copious natural energy cultivated in its many years on this earth.

◇ ◇ ◇

EVOLVING GENERATIONS
BREAKING FAMILY CYCLES

It is easy to believe that in leaving our childhood homes and embarking upon the journey of adulthood, we have effectively removed ourselves from harmful and self-perpetuating familial patterns. In looking closely at ourselves, however, we may discover that our behaviors and beliefs are still those that were impressed upon us during our youth by our parents, grandparents, and those who preceded them. We may find ourselves unconsciously perpetuating cycles of the previous generations, such as fear of not having enough, difficulty showing affection, and secrecy patterns.

The transmission of negative patterns from one generation to the next is not inevitable. It is possible to become the end point at which negative family cycles that have thrived for generations are exhausted and can exert their influence no longer. Breaking the pattern is a matter of overcoming those values imprinted upon us long ago in order to replace them with pure love, tolerance, and conscious awareness.

Even if you have struggled with the cumulative effects of family cycles that were an expression of established modes of living and a reflection of the strife your ancestors were forced to endure, you can still liberate yourself from being under their influence. The will to divest yourself of old dark forms of familial energy and carry forth a new loving energy may come by way of an epiphany: You could one day simply realize that certain aspects of your early life have negatively affected your health, happiness, and ability to evolve as an individual. Or you may find that in order to transcend long-standing patterns of limiting beliefs, irrational behavior, and emotional stiltedness, you have to question your values and earnestly examine how your family has impacted your personality. Only when you understand how generational cycles have influenced you can you gain freedom from them.

In order to truly change, you must give yourself permission to do so. Breaking family patterns is in no way an act of defiance or betrayal. It is important that you trust yourself implicitly when determining the behaviors and beliefs that will help you overwrite the generation-based cyclical value system that has limited your individual potential. Many people are on the earth at this time to break negative family cycles, for all of you are true pioneers. In disrupting these patterns, you will discover that your ability to express your feelings and needs grows exponentially and that you embark upon a journey toward greater well-being that can positively impact generations to come.

◇ ◇ ◇

HIDDEN GEMS
EXPERIENCES WE DON'T UNDERSTAND

Sometimes we have an experience that we don't understand — but if we look deeply, or wait long enough, a reason for that experience will usually reveal itself. All the events in our lives lead to other events, and all that we have manifested in this present moment is the result of past occurrences and experiences. We cannot easily tease apart the many threads that have been woven together to create our current reality. Experiences that do not make sense, as well as any that we regret, are just as responsible for the good things in our lives as those we do understand or label as good.

This is especially important to remember on occasions when we feel directionless or unsure of what to do. It is often at times such as these that we take a job or move to a place without really knowing if it is the right thing to do. We may ultimately end up leaving the job or the place, but often while we are there we will have met someone who becomes an important friend, or we may have an experience that changes us in a profound way. When all the pieces of our lives do not quite make sense, we can remember that there may be some hidden gem of a reason why we are where we are and are having the experiences we are having.

It is fun to look back on prior events with an eye to uncovering those gems—the dreadful temporary job in a bland office building that introduced you to the love of your life, the roommate you could not tolerate who gave you a book that changed your life, or the time spent living in a city you did not like that led you into a deeper relationship with yourself. Remembering these past experiences can restore your faith in the present. Life is full of buried treasures. Chances are, you are sitting on some right now.

◇ ◇ ◇

HIDDEN TREASURE
FINDING ANOTHER VANTAGE POINT

The ocean can look very different depending on whether you are standing at the shore, soaring above in a plane, or swimming beneath its waves. Likewise, a mountain can appear quite different relative to where you are standing. Each living thing sees the world from its unique vantage point. From your window you may observe what looks like a huge shrub, but a bird in its nest is getting an intimate view of that tree's leafy interior. Meanwhile, a beetle sees only a massive and never-ending trunk. Yet all three of you are looking at the same tree.

Just as a shadow that is concealed from one point of view is easily seen from another, it is possible to miss a fantastic sight—that is, unless you are willing to see what is in front of you through different eyes. Seeing the world from another perspective, whether spatially or mentally, can introduce you to all sorts of hidden treasures; and often this lies at the root of the discovery process. The common human reaction to arachnids is one example: Spinning its web in a dark corner, a spider may seem drab, frightening, and mysterious. But seen up close while it weaves silver snowflakes between the branches of a tree, it can look like a colored jewel.

Sometimes there are experiences in life that from your vantage point may seem confusing, alarming, or worrisome . . . or there may be events that look insignificant from where you are standing right now. Try seeing them from another point of view. Bury your face in the grass and look at the world from a bug's perspective. Explore your home as if you were a small child. Take a ride in a small aircraft and experience the world from a bird's-eye view. Just as kneeling down sometimes helps you see more closely when you are searching for lost treasure, so, too, can standing back help you appreciate the broader picture of what you are looking at. In doing so, you will experience very different worlds.

◇ ◇ ◇

MAKE IT SO
CREATIVE-VISUALIZATION TECHNIQUES

Athletes do it, business executives do it, and children do it without even realizing how powerful it is. It is called *visualization,* and the concept is simple: being able to enhance or change your reality by using your imagination. You may not realize it, but you probably already practice some type of visualization. Reality follows idea, and most of the time the process is so seamless that you take it for granted. It is a smaller step than you might imagine to get from picturing and then executing an excellent golf swing to imagining your next job into reality, or improving your progress by conceiving what your life will be like when you reach a fitness goal or a spiritual milestone. Many people have substantially transformed their lives by setting the change in their mind's eye before making it happen.

To use visualization to enhance your life and help you achieve your goals, it is important to be clear about what you desire. You may want to start small for practice, but it is essential that you not doubt your ability to manifest your dreams. Include all the details of what you wish for—set them in your mind, or even write them down.

After you are sure about your goals, create a soothing environment to begin your visualization. It is important to fully relax and allow your imagination to go to work. Shake out any tension in your body; then close your eyes and take some deep breaths. Allow yourself to slow down more with each breath until you are completely serene. Picture yourself in the situation you desire. See it in the present tense and allow all of your senses to experience the image. How does it look, feel, taste, and smell? Imagine any positive emotions that are part of the situation—this is no time to let any potential roadblocks get in your way.

Practice visualizing your heart's desire often, perhaps even once or twice a day. It does not have to be for a long time; even a few minutes of vivid imagery is powerful. Also, feel free to visit the image casually as you go about your day.

While it is valuable to practice visualization frequently, the irony is that you also have to trust in, and be relaxed about, your potential situation coming to fruition. In other words, you want to be consistent in your imagery, but you do not want to be obsessive. When the subject of your visualization is manifested, be sure to acknowledge your part in achieving it, yet be grateful to the universe as well for allowing reality to meet your dreams.

◇ ◇ ◇

THE GREAT TRANSFORMER
LOVING WHAT YOU HATE

Hatred can be irrational, and it has a greater impact on the individual who hates than the person or object being hated. Overcoming this negative feeling is difficult because it reinforces itself and causes greater enmity to come into being. The most powerful tool you can use to combat it is love. Deciding to love what you hate — whether this is a person, a situation, or a part of yourself — can create a profound change in your feelings and your experience. There is little time for anger, dislike, bitterness, or resentment when you are busy loving what you hate. The practice of doing so can transform and shift your emotions from loathing to caring, because there is no room for hatred in a space occupied by love.

Granted, it is difficult to forgo judging someone, to love your enemy, and to seek the good in situations that seem orchestrated to cause you pain or anger. But in deciding to love what you hate, you become one less person adding negativity to the universe. On a simple level, this can help you enjoy your life more. On a more complex level, you are set free because you disengage yourself from the hatred that can weigh down the soul.

Responding with love to people radiating hatred transmutes their harmful energy. You also empower yourself by not letting their negativity enter your personal space. Rather than lowering yourself to the level of their hatred, you give the other person an opportunity to rise above his or her feelings and meet you on the field of love.

Gandhi once said, "We must be the change we wish to see in the world." Loving what you hate sends a positive, beautiful energy to people while spreading peace and harmony throughout the planet. Instead of reinforcing conflict, you become an advocate for caring. Hatred responds to hate by causing anguish but responds to love by transforming into blissful peace.

◇ ◇ ◇

PERMANENTLY PARENTS
THE CHANGING NEST

Once individuals become parents, they are parents for-evermore. Their identities change perceptibly the moment Mother Nature inaugurates them Mom or Dad. However, the role they undertake when they welcome children into their lives is not a fixed one. As children move from one phase of their lives to the next, parental roles change. When these transitions involve a child gaining independence, many parents experience an empty-nest feeling. Instead of being proud that he or she has achieved so much—whether the flight from the nest refers to the first day of kindergar-ten or the start of college—they feel that they are losing a part of themselves. However, when approached thought-fully, this new stage of parental life can be an exciting time in which mothers and fathers rediscover themselves and relate to children in a new way.

As children earn greater levels of independence, their parents often gain unanticipated freedom. Used to being depended upon by their sons and daughters and subject to their demands, parents sometimes forget that they are not only Mom or Dad, but also individuals. As the nest empties, they can alleviate the anxiety and sadness they feel by rediscovering themselves and honoring the immense strides their children have made in life.

The simplest way to honor a child undergoing a transition is to allow that child to make decisions and choices appropriate to his or her level of maturity. Freed from the role of disciplinarian, parents of college-age children can befriend their offspring and undertake an advisory position. Those with younger ones beginning school or teenagers taking a first job can plan a special day in which they express their pride and explain that they will always be there to offer love and support.

An empty nest can touch other members of the family unit as well. Young people may feel isolated or abandoned when their siblings leave the nest. Since this is normal, extra attention can help them feel more secure in their less-populated home. Spouses with more leisure time on their hands may need to relearn how to be best friends and lovers. Other family members will likely grieve less when they understand the significance of the child's new phase of life.

The more parents both celebrate and honor these transitions, the less apprehension the children will feel. Mothers and fathers who embrace their changing nest while still cherishing their offspring can look forward to developing deeper, more mature relationships with them in the future.

◇ ◇ ◇

FRESH AND UNFIXED
THERE IS ONLY NOW

It can be easy for us to walk through the world and our lives without really being present. While dwelling on the past and living for the future are common pastimes, it is physically impossible to live anywhere but the current moment. We cannot step out our front door and take a left turn to May of last year any more than we can make a right turn into the future. Nevertheless, we can easily miss the future we are waiting for because it has become the now we are too busy to pay attention to. We then spend the rest of our time playing catch-up to the moment we just let pass by. On occasions such as these, it is necessary to remember that there is only now.

In order to feel more at home in the present moment, it is important to try to stay aware, open, and receptive. Being in the now requires our complete attention so that we are fully awake to experience it. When we are wholly present, our minds do not wander. We are focused on what is going on right now rather than thinking about what just happened or worrying about what is going to happen next. Being present lets us experience each moment in our lives in a way that cannot be fully lived through memory or fantasy.

When we begin to corral our attention into the present moment, it can be almost overwhelming to be *here*. There is a state of stillness that has to happen that can take some getting used to, and the mind chatter that so often gets us into our heads and out of the present moment must be quieted. We may feel a lack of control because we are not busy planning our next move, assessing our current situation, or anticipating the future. Instead, being present requires that we be flexible, creative, attentive, and spontaneous. Each moment is completely new, and nothing like it has taken place before or ever will again.

As you move through your day, remember to stay present in each moment. In doing so, you will live without having to wait for the future or yearn for the past. Life happens to us when *we* happen to it in the now.

◇ ◇ ◇

WHY ME?

PITY PARTY

We all have days when the bad things seem to outweigh the good, and we begin to think that life is not fair. We get stuck in traffic, which makes us late for an important meeting, and then our car gets towed. We might ask ourselves, *Why me?*

Events such as these can test anyone's ability to be grateful and feel optimistic. If you have a tendency to feel sorry for yourself—and many of us do—things usually progress to the next stage: the pity party. You begin to feel like the innocent victim of a dismal fate because you are seeing your life through inaccurate lenses. Most of the thoughts that run through your mind at times like these are not helpful, and they mainly serve to increase your indignation and sense of powerlessness. What these feelings and thoughts *do not* do is change your circumstances or make you feel better.

When you have a terrible day, there should definitely be a time and place to experience your feelings so that you can process them. It is important not to pretend that you are fine with things when you are not. It is also important, however, to notice when you are having a pity party. It is a good idea to set a time limit in which to fully express your emotions and not to feel guilty, be ashamed, or judge yourself. Having a friend witness you during this process can be helpful. You may also want to write about how you feel. When your time is up, let go of the negativity you just expressed. You can declare your intention to your companion. If you have written down your feelings, you can burn the piece of paper or throw it in the recycling bin.

Try not to dwell on unpleasant experiences, and do everything you can to avoid holding on to negative emotions. When you indulge in self-pity, you only make a bad day worse. Try to stop feeling sorry for yourself, release the notion that you are a victim, and notice the good that exists in your life.

◇ ◇ ◇

IN ALL KINDS OF WEATHER
BEING HAPPY FOR FRIENDS

When we are close friends with someone, we intuitively know when they need a hug, a helping hand, or a sympathetic ear. Likewise, when we are going through bleak periods in our lives, we count on others to support us through loss, illness, and other setbacks, both big and small. And while part of being a good friend means being there when other people need us, it is just as important to be there to share in their joyous celebrations and triumphs.

After all, who else would our friends want to celebrate their promotions, graduations, marriages, and good news with than their loved ones, including *us*. Yet depending on what is happening in our lives, it can sometimes be difficult to be there for our friends during the good times. We can become so busy that we forget to make time. Or we may be so focused on our own problems that we might not feel like celebrating with our friends. We may even take their joyful moments for granted, assuming that as long as we are there for them during the bad times, we are doing our jobs. Part of being a true friend, however, means also being there during the *good* times. Success and happiness can feel empty without someone to share them with, and who better to join in our victory dances than our close friends.

Taking the time from our busy lives to honor our friends' happy moments is a wonderful way to show them that they matter. Also, in many ways, by wanting us around during their happy occasions, our friends are also honoring *us*. After all, it is the people we cherish whom we want to sing at our birthdays, visit our newborn babies, and pop open that bottle of champagne when we reach a milestone.

The next time a friend wants you to be there for such a moment, remember to feel honored that the person thought of asking you. Together, you can celebrate his or her happiness and your rich friendship.

◇ ◇ ◇

FOLLOWING THE CURRENT
GOING WITH THE FLOW

The expression "Go with the flow" is a metaphor that applies to navigating a river. When we go with the flow, we follow the current of the water rather than pushing against it. People who go with the flow may be interpreted as lazy or passive; but to truly do so requires awareness, presence, and the ability to blend one's own energy with the prevailing energy. Going with the flow does not mean that we toss our oars into the water and kick back in the boat, hoping for the best; rather, it means that we let go of our individual agenda and notice the play of energy all around us. We tap into that force and yield to it, which gets us where we need to go a whole lot faster than resistance will.

Going with the flow does not imply that we don't know where we are headed, but simply that we are open to multiple ways of getting there. We are also willing to change our destination, clinging more to the essence of our goal than to the particulars. We acknowledge that letting go and modifying our plans is part of the process. Going with the flow means that we are aware of an energy that is larger than our small selves and are open to working with it, not against it.

Many of us are afraid of going with the flow because we do not trust that we will get where we want to be if we do. This causes us to cling to plans that are not working, stick to routes that are obstructed, and obsess over relationships that are not fulfilling.

When you find yourself stuck in these kinds of patterns, do yourself a favor and open to the flow of what is rather than resisting it. Trust that the big river of your life has a plan for you, and let it carry you onward. Throw overboard those things that are weighing you down. Be open to revising your maps. Take a deep breath and move into the current.

◇ ◇ ◇

LIVING EXPLORATION
DISCOVERING WHAT YOU WANT
THROUGH EXPERIENCE

The road to knowing what you want is often paved with many moments of learning what you do *not* want. This holds true in all areas of life, from work to love. Recognizing and accepting this fact can give you the courage to keep moving forward when you might otherwise paralyze yourself through fear of making a wrong move.

All too often we expect ourselves to know in advance what will or will not work. But this is like accepting an invitation from a new dance partner only if we are sure that we will want to dance with that person forever. We need to accept the invitation without knowing where it will lead us. When we do so, what we are committing to is exploration.

It helps to remember that decisions are not permanent or final actions. They are just the first steps in an unfolding process of inquiry. Many people go to school for one thing and end up on a completely different career path. This does not mean that they made a mistake in studying English literature and then becoming a nurse. One thing leads to another in ways we cannot always foresee.

Try to remain open and curious along the way, asking questions: *How does this feel? How could it be better? What changes can be made to improve the situation?* With each modification, you move closer to creating exactly what you want. Just remember that sometimes you need to experience what you do not want to determine what you *do* want.

◇ ◇ ◇

GRATEFUL LIVING
HOME AND LAND MEDITATION

Just as we take care of our friends and families, our homes and Mother Earth take care of us. Our homes give us a place of refuge—a sanctuary that stands between us and the elements of nature and the rest of the world. The earth is an unselfish giver of life and the steward of our physical and spiritual needs. Her bountiful plant life nourishes us, gives us air, and offers us cooling shade. Her waters quench our thirst, and her beauty stirs our souls.

Yet it is easy to take both of these wonderful sources of blessings for granted. Expressing the gratitude you feel toward your home and the earth for what each provides can help you stay conscious of where many of the gifts in your life come from. Each time you give thanks, you will be reminded of the importance of caring for your home and for Mother Earth. There is a simple and beautiful meditation you can perform to show your gratitude.

Begin by finding a quiet place where you can be alone. Sit comfortably and breathe deeply until you feel relaxed, and then read the following out loud:

"Thank you, home, for allowing me to live within your walls. Thank you for giving me shelter, warmth, and security. Thank you for allowing me to live my life in your womb, for staying strong and sturdy, for supporting me, and for your beauty.

"Thank you, Earth, for the land that I live on and for allowing me to steward life with you. Thank you for allowing me to walk upon your soil, cultivate you, and live in partnership with you. Thank you for supporting my home and my family.

"Thank you, plants, minerals, and animals that dwell on the land that I steward. Thank you for allowing me to experience your beauty and share in the wonderment of life and for the honor of living with all of you on this earth. Thank you for the wisdom and joy you bring to humanity.

"I honor you."

You can perform this meditation as often as you like and anytime you feel particularly thankful for the many blessings that you have received. Each time you do, you will reaffirm and strengthen your connection with all that protects, supports, and sustains you.

◇ ◇ ◇

PERMISSION TO FEEL
PUSHING AWAY EMOTIONS

Throughout our lives, we may experience emotions that disturb or distress us. Often our first reaction is to push them away. We may say, "I don't want to think about that right now—I'll think about it later," and we bury our feelings, deny their validity, or distract ourselves with other concerns.

The diverse emotions you experience are neither good nor bad—they are simply a part being human. Choosing not to face pain, anger, or other intense feelings could cause them to become buried deep into your physical body. There, they may linger unresolved and unable to emerge, even as they affect the way you experience the world. Allowing yourself to experience all of your emotions, rather than pushing the more painful ones away, can help you come to terms with them so that you can process them and then move on.

It is possible to bring forth the old feelings you have pushed aside and experience them in a safe and enriching way. It may sound silly to set aside time to feel your old wounds that you have not dealt with, but this can be a very beneficial healing experience.

Find a safe place, and pick a time when you can be alone. Make sure that you feel secure and comfortable in your surroundings. Bring to mind the circumstances that originally triggered the emotions you have been pushing away. You may need to revisit these circumstances by reading relevant entries in your journal or using visualization to relive your past.

Once you have triggered your long-denied feelings, let yourself experience them, and try not to judge your reactions. Cry or sound your emotions if you need to, and do not block their flow. Allow any thoughts that are connected to them to surface. As you release the feelings you have pushed inside of you, you will find yourself healing from the experience associated with them.

When you deal with your feelings directly, they can move through you rather than staying stopped up in your body as emotional blocks that can sometimes turn into disease. Acknowledging your feelings instead of pushing them away allows you to stay healthy and in touch with yourself emotionally.

◇ ◇ ◇

HEALING THE PAST
FIRE-HEALING MEDITATION

Each of us has unresolved issues about our relationships that linger in our soul. People do not always say or do what is right, and it can seem impossible to heal that breach, particularly when those involved are unresponsive or have passed away.

The following fire meditation is a way to release pain and heal a past or present relationship or deal with unresolved interpersonal issues. Through this type of exercise, it becomes possible to seek out reconciliation and forgiveness, as well as rid yourself of the spiritual baggage that can come when you harbor emotional pain.

During this meditation, it can be helpful to have a partner who reads the instructions to you in a soothing voice. Or, if you prefer to meditate alone, you may want to record yourself reading them and play the tape when you are ready to start.

Begin by finding a quiet, relaxing space. In choosing, you should bear in mind that you will want to keep your back as straight as possible, either by lying down on a flat surface or sitting upright in a chair. Breathe deeply and relax your body and mind.

When you have reached a state of deep relaxation, envision the place where you feel most safe. It need not be a real location; it can be an isolated private island, a tropical beach, or a mountain sanctuary. It can even be your own bedroom. Take the time to really see and experience your safe place. Smell the air, listen for sounds, and feel the ground under you.

When you are relaxed in your surroundings, envision a road. Look down it and watch for the arrival of whomever you wish to make peace with. Let this person or animal come at any pace, and when your visitor is in full view, ask if your companion is willing to heal with you. If the answer is yes, look at yourself first. How old are you? What are you wearing? How old is your companion, and what does the person or animal look like?

The next step is to envision a fire. It can be in any form you wish: a campfire, a ceremonial blaze, or a bonfire. As you begin to heal, throw your baggage into the flames and ask for forgiveness or for the closure you are seeking. If you wish, you can step into the fire; it will not harm you. Release everything that you no longer desire for yourself or your companion into the fire. In doing so, you may feel your body temperature rise, or you may shake a little. This is normal. Take as much time as you need with your companion.

When you are finished, release your visitor to turn and walk back down the road. Stay in your safe place for as long as you desire. When you feel comfortable, open your eyes and note that a great weight has been lifted from you.

◇ ◇ ◇

SEEING DIFFERENTLY
CHANGING YOUR PERSPECTIVE

Some people have a knack for looking at a scene or situation and perceiving things not only in terms of their own experiences, but also in terms of others'. They embrace changes in perspective and look at things from many vantage points. Other people, however, see what they see and may not be convinced that someone else might view things differently.

A shift in perspective can be a valuable tool in interacting with others, remaining open to new ideas, and increasing creativity. Your point of view normally reflects a reality that is uniquely yours. But think of viewing a room from two different angles — you will see different items depending on your position. Or consider the difference between looking out over the rolling ocean versus seeing into its depths while snorkeling.

Most people have at one time or another tried looking at a situation through someone else's eyes. Changing your perspective can be applied to many different circumstances. For example, you might try seeing the disappointment of not having funds to travel as an opportunity to more deeply explore activities offered in your own neighborhood. When you are faced with a challenge, attempt to view the problem from all angles in order to solve it. You will be more likely to come up with a novel solution. Changing how you perceive enhances objectivity while refreshing creativity. In fact, it is said that the most creative people see what everyone else does but look at life in ways most do not. Try finding the angular beauty in a cityscape or the opportunities for fun on a wet, dreary day. They are there.

The universe is a vast conglomeration of all perspectives. Changing or expanding yours is not about avoiding another viewpoint or ignoring the parts of life you find unpleasant. Everything that exists continues to do so whether you choose to focus on it or not. Rather, a shift in perception can help you understand the world in a different way — from a new angle — so that you can solve problems, create things of beauty, and lead the life you truly desire.

◇ ◇ ◇

SPREADING YOUR LIGHT
HOW YOU AFFECT OTHERS DAILY

As the pace and fullness of modern life serve to isolate us from one another, the contact we do share becomes vastly more significant. We unconsciously absorb each other's energy, adopting the temperament of those with whom we share close quarters, and we find ourselves changed after the briefest encounters. Everything we do or say has the potential to affect not only the individuals we live, work, and play with, but also those we have just met. Although we may never know the impact we have had or the scope of our influence, accepting and understanding that our attitudes and choices will touch others can help us remember to conduct ourselves with grace at all times. When we seek always to be friendly, helpful, and responsive, we effortlessly create an atmosphere around ourselves that is both uplifting and inspiring.

Most people rarely give thought to the effect they have had or will have on others. When we take a few moments to contemplate how our individual modes of being affect the people we spend time with each day, we come one step closer to seeing ourselves through the eyes of others. By asking ourselves whether those we encounter walk away feeling appreciated, respected, and liked, we can heighten our awareness of the effect we ultimately have.

Something as simple as a smile given freely can temporarily brighten a person's entire world. Our value-driven conduct may inspire others to consider whether their own lives are reflective of their values. A word of advice can help people see everything in an entirely new fashion, and small gestures of kindness can even prove to those embittered by the world that goodness still exists. By simply being ourselves, we influence others in both subtle and life-altering ways.

To ensure that the effect we have is positive, we must strive to stay true to ourselves while realizing that it is the demeanor we project and not the quality of our wondrous inner landscapes that people see. Thus, as we interact with others, how we behave can be as important as who we are. If we project our passion for life, our warmth, and our tolerance in our facial features, voice, and choice of words, all who enter our circle of influence will leave our presence feeling at peace with themselves and with us.

You never know whose life you are affecting, in a big or small way. Try to remember this as you go out into the world each day.

◇ ◇ ◇

YOU ARE WHO YOU ARE, NOT WHAT YOU DO
BECOMING YOUR "WRONG" DECISIONS

Our perception of the traits and characteristics that make us who we are is often tightly intertwined with how we live our life. We define ourselves in terms of the roles we adopt, our actions and *in*actions, our triumphs, and what we think are failures. As a result, it is easy to identify so strongly with a decision that has brought on unexpected negative consequences that we actually *become* that "wrong" decision. The disappointment and shame we feel when we commit what we perceive to be a mistake grows until it becomes a dominant part of our identities. We rationalize our "poor" choices by labeling ourselves incompetent decision makers.

However, your true identity cannot be defined by your choices. Your essence — what makes you a unique entity — exists independently of your decision-making process. There are no true right or wrong decisions; *all* contribute to your development and are an integral part of your evolving existence, yet are still separate from the self. A decision that does not result in its intended outcome is in no way an illustration of character. Still, it can have dire effects on your self-esteem and ability to trust yourself.

You can avoid becoming your decisions by affirming that a "bad" one was just an experience, and next time you can choose differently. Try to refrain from lingering in the past and mulling over the circumstances that led to your perceived error in judgment. Instead, adapt to the new circumstances you must face by considering how you can use your intelligence, inner strength, and intuition to aid you in moving forward more mindfully. Try not to entirely avoid thinking about the choices you have made, but reflect on their consequences from a rational rather than an emotional standpoint. Strive to understand why you made the decision you did, forgive yourself, and then move forward.

A perceived mistake becomes a valuable learning experience and is, in essence, a gift of growth. You are not a bad person, and you are not your decisions; you are simply human.

◇ ◇ ◇

YOU ARE WHAT YOU SPEAK
POWER OF WORDS

Words have power. Despite the reassurances of the old childhood rhyme "Sticks and stones may break my bones, but words will never hurt me," we all know that words *can* hurt. Hopefully, most of us try to refrain from saying injurious things, but we can take a step further on the path to enlightenment by being conscious of the words we use—which means becoming aware of their power and the energy behind them.

Speaking consciously is very effective in bringing about positive change. You can actually transform your life for the better by being more aware of the things you say. For instance, if you are constantly putting yourself down, saying "I'm fat, clumsy, unpopular [. . . and so on]," then you will no doubt feel as such. However, if you stroke yourself with positive affirmations such as "I am fit, athletic, and friendly," you will feel more positive about yourself and aspire to such admirable qualities.

Having an upbeat attitude and being aware of our words is equally important when speaking to others. Everyone knows how draining it is to be around those who complain or gossip all the time. However, we are drawn like magnets to cheerful people who are free with compliments or make us laugh.

Be conscious of your words and your intentions in speaking. Speak truthfully so that you truly mean and feel what you say. Try to be fully aware of those you are talking to and the effect of your words on them; this way, you will be less likely to speak negatively.

◇ ◇ ◇

A SEPARATE REALITY
DISCONNECTING FROM THE SOURCE

We all experience periods when we feel separated from the loving ebb and flow of the universe. These times of disconnectedness from the source may occur for many reasons, but self-sabotage is the most common cause. We purposely, although often unconsciously, cut ourselves off from the flow of the universe and from the embrace of humanity so that we can avoid dealing with painful issues, shun the necessary steps for growth, or prevent the success that we are afraid of achieving from ever happening.

When you choose to disconnect from the source, you block the flow of the universe's energy from passing through you. You become like a sleepwalker who is not fully awake to life; and your hopes, plans, and dreams begin to appear as distant blurs on a faraway horizon. Universal support has never left you, but if you can remember that you became disconnected from source by choice, you can *choose* to *re*connect.

Tuning back in to the universe grounds you and is as easy as your making a concerted effort to become interested in the activities you love or responding to what nurtures or stimulates you. You may also want to make a list of the pursuits and kinds of experiences that touch your soul. Try to pinpoint the times when you have felt fully engaged and aware, and ask yourself what you were doing. But one of the simplest ways to reconnect is simply stating the intention of doing so.

When you disengage from the universe, your sense of purpose, creativity, and ability to be innovative are not as easy to access. You may also experience a deep, empty longing or feel devoid of ideas or unworthy of love. It is important, however, to recognize that being disconnected from the source is never a permanent state, and it can be reversed anytime you decide that you are ready. When you are connected back to the universe, all aspects of your being will feel alive as its flow pours through you and into your life.

◇ ◇ ◇

THE MIRRORING WORLD
WE ARE LIKE NATURE

Nature is a mirror, inspiring us, teaching us, and deepening our sense of belonging in the world. Wherever we look, we can see that our patterns and those of the natural world are the same. We can find this resonance in every form—from molecules, to plants and animals, to planets. We live our lives according to the same principles as the trees, the mountains, the clouds, and the birds.

We begin life in the womb, folded in on ourselves like the bud of a flower. We can see our whole lives in the mirror of this natural form. When we emerge from the womb, we slowly commence our unfolding, just as the flower begins to open its petals. At its prime, the blossom draws many insects to it and also the eyes of appreciative humans. When its petals begin to fade and its life cycle comes to an end, it ceases to hold itself upright and returns to the earth. Traditionally, so do we, just as all plants and animals do. Like flowers, we leave behind seeds in the form of children and other gifts only we could have given, which continue to unfold even after we are gone. Rebirth is encoded into our lives, and death is just one part of the cycle.

Look around and you will find connection and insight. Notice how your moods shift from one to another like the sky transitions from bright blue to turbulent grays. Your thoughts are akin to clouds: appearing, changing shape, passing through, and then disappearing without a trace. The rain cleanses the sky, just as an emotional release cleanses your mind. The sky itself is your eternal awareness, unchanging underneath all these permutations. Let it reflect back to you your own abiding perfection.

As you walk through the world, find your own metaphors for connectedness in nature. Flesh them out fully, and follow them as they lead you through the mystery and intelligence of life.

◇ ◇ ◇

THE POWER OF EMPATHY
BEING AFRAID OF OPENING YOUR HEART

It is not easy to have an open heart in a world that offers us a full plate of experiences. This life gives us much joy, love, and light; but it also shows us a fair amount of pain, sadness, and suffering. When our hearts are open, we take everything into ourselves and we are deeply affected by what we see. We do not hold ourselves separate from the pain of others. In addition, our own personal disappointments may begin to take their toll. We may feel small, alone, and overwhelmed. Most of us might not think we are up to the task of living with our hearts open; and we could begin to close down, little by little, so that we can get through our days without having to feel too much.

One thing that can help us turn this situation around is an awareness of the power of empathy. To open ourselves up to another person's suffering is a revolutionary act that has energetic implications. Many experiments with meditation have proven that we can reach far beyond the boundaries of our selves and heal others when our hearts are open. A heart meditation awakens this power and heals the person meditating as well as anyone who is its focus.

You may want to experiment with this the next time you see or hear something painful. Instead of shutting down your emotions, resolve to hold your feelings in your heart. Tap into the divine energy of universal love that resides within you. This energy makes you powerful, for it is your protection that will transmute the hurt of others. Breathe deeply and let yourself feel the pain of the situation, knowing that your heart is big and strong enough to hold it. As you breathe, visualize healing light emanating from your core and touching all who are suffering. You will heal *your* heart in the process.

◇ ◇ ◇

THE GRASS IS ALWAYS GREENER
FINDING THE JOY YOU HAVE

Not one life goes by in which the quest for joy and happiness is absent. It is unfortunate, however, that people so often believe that the search will be entirely fulfilled by finding the perfect job, acquiring some new gadget, losing weight, or maintaining an image. The problem inherent in looking outward for sources of happiness is that focusing on what you *do not* have or what you are *not* inevitably leads to *un*happiness.

It is easy to get caught up in your desires and to ignore the sources of joy and growth already present in your life. It is said that the grass is always greener on the other side of the fence. When you have stopped comparing yourself and your assets to others, you will be able to recognize that, to others, you *are* on the "greener side." Learning to live in the moment and enjoy your personal lot can be a source of profound contentment.

Start by recognizing what you have. List 100 reasons you have to be thankful, even if they seem like small things. Your emotions are based on your perspective, so try to envision a circumstance in which your reasons feel important; then apply that perspective. Joy and satisfaction must come from the inside. Many people feel very sincerely that a different job, financial situation, or wardrobe would bring them happiness, only to find out when they have achieved their goal that they feel the same as they did before. Accepting your current circumstances and embracing them rather than expending energy on negative thinking will help you overcome obstacles and enact changes naturally. The happier you are, the more you will be able to make the positive changes that really matter.

Unhappiness inspired by what you do not have is easy to overcome when you open your eyes to the wonderful things already present in your life. Remember that joy is a state of mind, and it is pointless to sacrifice the happiness of today for a set of possibilities that may or may not come to be.

◇ ◇ ◇

CLEANING MORE
THAN JUST CLUTTER
THE BENEFITS OF SPACE CLEARING

Everyone has had the experience of walking into a room, building, or home that just feels good. Likewise, there are spaces that make us feel uncomfortable for no apparent reason. We can attribute some of our feelings to the environment. Someplace clean and spacious with nice furniture and pleasant artwork is obviously more appealing than a dark, cluttered room. What we are reacting to is actually more than just the physical surroundings. On an intuitive level, we pick up on the energy of any area we enter.

This is why space clearing can be so valuable, especially in your own home. This activity is more than just spring-cleaning or getting rid of clutter, although those are important first steps. It is a ceremony that frees your home of old energy, which is particularly important after someone has been ill or if there has been an argument in one of the rooms. You will notice an immediate difference after a space clearing; and you may even see an improvement in relationships, finances, or health issues.

There are recommended steps for a space-clearing ceremony. Some are more involved than others, but they basically follow the same principle of *intention*. It is good to begin with a thorough physical cleaning and to get rid of clutter. Think about what your intentions are for your home and what you want to invite into your life. You may want to create a quiet, relaxed atmosphere; or you may want your home to be full of people and laughter. The more focused you are about your vision, the easier it is to manifest the home of your dreams.

To begin clearing, go from room to room and sense the energy throughout the house. You may find that some areas feel more stagnant than others and you will know then that you will need to spend more time and energy clearing them. To do so, you may drum, clap, or ring a bell or chime. You may also burn a sage smudge throughout the entire house, being sure to reach into corners, inside closets, and under beds.

These are steps for a quick energy tune-up:

1. Start with a thorough cleaning.

2. Allow sunlight and fresh air into your space on a daily basis, or bring in a few fresh plants (be sure to water them and keep them healthy).

3. Do an abbreviated clapping or chime ringing in areas where the energy seems heavy.

You will be surprised how much better you and your home will feel.

◇ ◇ ◇

BEARERS OF WISDOM
THE ELDERLY

In tribal cultures, the elderly play an important role. They are the keepers of the group's memories and the holders of wisdom. As such, they are honored and respected members of the tribe. In many modern cultures, however, this is often not the case. Many older people say that they feel ignored, left out, and disrespected. This is a sad commentary on modernization, but we can change this situation by taking the time to examine our attitudes about the elderly and then taking action.

Modern societies tend to be obsessed with the ideas of newness, youth, and progress. Scientific studies tell us how to do everything—from the way we should raise our kids to what we need to eat for breakfast. As a result, the wisdom that is passed down from older generations is often disregarded. Of course, grandparents and retirees have more than information to offer the world. Their maturity and experience allow for a larger perspective of life, and we can learn a lot from talking to them.

It is a shame that society does not do more to allow the older population to continue to feel productive for the rest of their lives, but *you* can help make change. Perhaps you could facilitate a mentorship program that would allow children to be tutored by the residents in retirement homes. The elderly make wonderful storytellers, and creating programs where they can share their real-life experiences with others is another way to educate and inspire other generations.

Take stock of your relationships with members of the elderly population. Maybe you do not really listen to them because you hold the belief that their time has passed, and they are too old to understand what you are going through. You may even realize that you do not have any relationships with older people. Try to understand why and how cultural perceptions of the elderly influence the way you perceive them. Look around you and reach out to someone who is in their later years, even if you are just saying hello and making small talk. Resolve to be more aware of the elderly. They are our mentors, wise folk, and the pioneers who came before us and paved the way for our future.

◇ ◇ ◇

WORKING THROUGH
HARD DAYS

We all have days that seem endlessly difficult and hard—when it is as if the odds are stacked against us, and we just cannot get a break as one challenging situation follows another. We may feel as though we were standing in the ocean being hit by wave after wave, never able to get a full breath. Sometimes it is necessary or worth it to stay in the fray and work our way through. Other times, the best idea is to go home and take the breath we need in order to carry on.

If the only choice is to get through it, a hard day can be a great teacher. It *will* eventually end; and we can look back on it, taking pride in the stamina, courage, and ingenuity it took to hold our ground. In hindsight, we may also see how we could have done things differently. This knowledge will be valuable when we face hard days in the future.

As we are deciding whether to work through it, we must trust our gut and know that sometimes a timely retreat is the best way to ensure a positive outcome. Getting space can remind us that external circumstances are not the whole picture. Once we catch our breath and recenter ourselves, we will be able to determine our next move. With a little perspective, we may even find the inner resources to change our attitude toward what is happening and begin to see that what we viewed as hardships are actually opportunities. As our outlook changes for the better, our actions and the circumstances will follow suit.

Sometimes all that is needed is a good night's sleep. No one is immune to having a hard day, and these are usually the times we can learn the most. If we can find it in our hearts to examine the day and maybe make a single small change in perception, we can ease our pain and greet the next one that much wiser.

◇ ◇ ◇

BEING TRULY FREE
LETTING GO

There is tremendous freedom in letting go. It is liberation to rid ourselves of things that clutter our lives—too many possessions, useless emotions, unhealthy habits, old beliefs, and even people who drain our energy. All these things and more can weigh us down. Every once in a while it is good to "clean out our closets," literally and figuratively.

Like pruning dead branches or a snake shedding an old skin, we need to let go of what no longer serves or fits us so that there is room for something new, alive, and vital for *this* time in our lives. Yet we are a possessive society. We often hold on to things, feelings, and relationships out of habit or, many times, out of fear of being without. So much of learning to let go is about developing trust. We have to be able to trust that, indeed, new branches will grow, and that there is a new skin under the old one. And to the degree that we are willing to let go, we are able to receive. When we stop clinging to anything, we realize we have *every*thing.

In reality, we really own nothing — and certainly not people. Our spouse, boy- or girlfriend, and children are not truly "ours." Even if we own the title to our house or car, such possessions can be gone in a moment, taken by a natural disaster, an accident, or financial circumstances. Native Americans could not grasp the European concept of proprietorship of land, any more than owning the sky — for everything belongs to the universe, as even we do. When we allow ourselves to rethink our sense of ownership, it is easier to let go. We no longer need to feel burdened by the responsibility of having to hold on to something.

Reassess the value of a prized book collection, a coveted job, and feelings for an old flame. Perhaps it is not necessary to physically get rid of something; but letting go of the power that a person, ideology, or material object possesses is truly freeing.

◇ ◇ ◇

STEPS IN THE RIGHT DIRECTION
TOOLS FOR BALANCE

The drive to better yourself and your life is never ending. Therefore, it can be helpful to have useful tools for general everyday improvements in life. Whenever a need for change arises and whatever it is, open your toolbox and integrate one or more of the following into your life:

— Each day, ask the universe how you may be of service. Since all people are intimately connected with the universe at large, you both work for it and benefit from it. When you give to the universe with positive intentions, you naturally reap abundance. Instead of waiting for opportunities to be of service to present themselves, ask what assistance you may provide. Inquire each morning upon waking or meditating. Be assured that the universe will ask no more from you than you are equipped to give.

— **Cook with intention, and bless all you consume.** The life force and what nourishes the spirit are closely intertwined with what you take into your body. The art of cooking involves preparing foods mindfully and projecting positive energy into what you eat. And part of bringing out the life force is showing loving respect for the labor involved in the cultivation and preparation of food. Speak a simple blessing over every meal to reinforce your connection with the circle of life.

— **Do unto others.** Promoting unselfish love in your life involves expressing spontaneous and unprovoked kindness toward all people. Taking the time to be kind will make your life and those of others more enjoyable and fulfilling.

— **Take time to center yourself daily.** Both in moments of strife and of calm, remember to direct your focus inward for a few moments each day. Pay attention to your body, determine where you are retaining tension, and let it go. Breathe deeply, close your eyes, and slip into a brief period of meditation. Allow yourself to be stabilized and strengthened by the earth's energy. When you have found a calm place, open your eyes and offer gratitude before continuing your day.

— **Take time to enjoy the community of others.** Although easy to neglect in this busy world, fellowship is a joyful part of being alive. Make time to spend with close friends or people who share your interests. Remember that shared joys are increased while divided pain is lessened.

◇ ◇ ◇

LOSING IT
YOU ARE NOT CRAZY

Most of us feel a little crazy from time to time. Periods of high stress can make us feel as if we are losing it, as can being surrounded by people whose values are very different from our own. Breaking off a significant relationship and moving into a new life situation are other events that can cause us to feel off-kilter.

Circumstances such as these recur in our lives, and they naturally affect our mental stability. The symptoms of our "unbalanced" state of mind can range from having no recollection of putting our car keys where we eventually find them, to wondering if we are seeing things clearly when everyone around us seems to be in denial about what is going on right in front of their eyes. For most of us, the key to survival in these moments is to step back, take a deep breath, and regain our composure. Then we can decide what course of action to take.

Sometimes a time-out does the trick. We take a day off from whatever is making us feel crazy and, like magic, we feel in our right mind again. Talking to an objective friend can also help. We begin to see what it is about the situation that destabilizes us, and we can make changes from there. At other times, if what we are facing is particularly sticky, we may need to seek professional help. Meeting with someone who understands the way the human mind reacts to stress, loss, and difficulties can make us feel less alone and more supported. Therapists or spiritual counselors can give us techniques that help bring us back to a sane state of mind so that we can effect useful change. They can also mirror our basic goodness, helping us see that we are actually okay.

The main purpose of the wake-up call that feeling crazy provides is to let you know that something in your life is out of balance. Confirm for yourself that you are capable of creating a sane and peaceful reality for yourself. Try to remember that most people have felt as if they were losing it at one time or another. You deserve a life that helps you thrive. Try to take some steps today to help you achieve more balance and a little less craziness.

◇ ◇ ◇

NURTURING GROWTH
SPIRITUAL PARENTING

A parent's job is to prepare his or her children for life. One of the best gifts to give yours, then, is a sense of their spiritual selves. Nurturing a love and appreciation of themselves and their relation to the universe at large will serve them well as they travel through life—especially when the road gets rocky, as it often does. Show your children love, instill compassion in them, teach them acceptance, and encourage an open mind so that they may discover the divine within.

It begins with love, of course. Make sure that your children always feel cherished through words and touch. Allow for lots of cuddling and kisses, and continue hugs and loving touches even as they become aloof adolescents. Encourage your children to be loving, too . . . not just toward family and friends, but toward everyone. Let them know that they are connected to everything—humans, animals, the earth, and the stars. People who understand that we are all one are more empathetic and less likely to hate and hurt.

Instill a sense of responsibility and ownership in your children so that they may be good stewards of the earth and value life. Teach them to be grateful. Let them know that a rainbow is as much of a gift as a toy. Encourage them to express thanks for every small favor and to see the blessings even in life's challenges.

The hard knocks are easier to take when you can change your outlook. Inspire self-discipline through a spiritual practice in the form of yoga, martial arts, prayer, meditation, music, or the arts. Learning to focus and ground yourself is the best way of connecting to the divine and getting to know yourself. Children with a strong sense of themselves are better able to make wise choices, connect with others in a positive way, and avoid destructive behavior. Communicate constantly with your sons and daughters, perhaps starting the ritual of council once a week.

Also, allow your children to fail. Let them know that we become better people when we learn from our mistakes and that no one is perfect, including you. Just be there when they fall, and then encourage them to get up and fly.

◇ ◇ ◇

IT BEGINS WITH YOU
LEARNING TO LOVE YOURSELF

We have all heard it countless times before: "To experience true love, we first must love ourselves." No matter how it is stated, the importance of self-love is vital to becoming a healthy, whole human being. We are all children of the universe, created out of love. We accept and care about other people, animals, nature — all that comes from the same source we do. We, too, then are worthy of our own love. To honor ourselves with affection and acceptance is to honor the universe that created us.

Self-love is about fully embracing ourselves, realizing our strengths and accepting our flaws. It is not about being self-centered or self-absorbed, which is based on insecurity and not knowing oneself. True self-love is a guarantee that we will not succumb to such selfish pursuits, for if we truly cherish ourselves, we know that we do not need to be the best looking or most talented or have the most possessions.

When we love ourselves, we are able to give love freely to others without fear of being hurt or used. We value ourselves enough not to allow anyone to take advantage of us. And, when we are secure in our love of self, we attract that of others.

To learn to love yourself, treat yourself in the same way you treat those you care about. Be kind to yourself, giving yourself all that you need to be happy and healthy. Show yourself a good time by doing things you like. Eat well and take care of your body. Say nice things to yourself—compliment and praise yourself just as you would a friend, family member, or lover. Encourage yourself when you are feeling down.

And, most important, say the words that we all long to hear. Look in the mirror and tell yourself: "I love you." This can be difficult, but it is a powerful tool in acceptance and self-love. It may not be easy—you may feel foolish at first—but you can do it. Even if you do not feel the caring energy right away, keep doing it. Love yourself first and you will be able to truly love others and will be truly loved in return.

◇ ◇ ◇

WAITING IN THE WINGS
SPIRIT GUIDES

Sometimes we have a sense that someone is near, offering comfort or support just when we need it, even though there is no one visibly around. We may be having difficulty making an important decision when we are given a sign: Something catches our attention, a message in graffiti or a song on the radio, and we feel guided in making the right choice.

Our spirit guides are waiting in the wings to offer their assistance whenever we need it. Different from angels who watch over and protect us, spirit guides are just what their name implies—beings who guide us on our spiritual path. Often, they have lived earthly lives and are now able to share their wisdom and knowledge from another realm.

Spirit guides come in many forms. The "imaginary" friends children so often have may indeed be one type. They are the ever-constant playmate, always there to keep children company, especially when they are lonely, scared, or mad at the world. We have only to open ourselves to their presence as children do and they will offer their support.

We can invite our spirit guides into our lives through meditation or simply by petitioning them and being more spiritually aware. Guides rarely inject themselves into our lives without being asked, although they will try to get our attention at times, especially when we are in need. Sometimes if the guides are loved ones we were close to, they will surround us with the scent of their favorite perfume or a spice they often cooked with. Sounds are also often used to attract our attention—chimes or a familiar tune may run through our minds.

When we listen, our guides have much to tell us. They are here to help us learn, assisting us so that we, too, can grow in spirit as they have—for we may one day be spirit guides ourselves.

◇ ◇ ◇

A WARM REFUGE
BEST FRIENDS

By the time we reach adulthood, many of us have had the good fortune of meeting at least one best friend. If we have moved around or changed our life situation repeatedly, we may be lucky enough to have had several. Our best friend is often our earliest intimate peer relationship and can be a source of great warmth and connection throughout our lives. The details of best friendship change as we grow up and grow older, but the heart of it remains the same: Our best friends are a warm refuge where we feel free to fully be ourselves, to share our deepest secrets, to rest when we are tired, and to celebrate when we are happy — a place where we feel utterly welcome to give and receive that most precious of all gifts: love.

Most intimate relationships hit bumps from time to time, and one of the hallmarks of an enduring best friendship is its ability to ride out the turbulence and remain intact even as it faces changes. Our most intimate friends are those who manage to love us through all of our transitions, just as we do for them. We find ways to embrace and appreciate the differences that set us apart and offer love and support no matter what. We allow each other to be exactly as we are at a given moment, even as we permit each other to change over time. In this way, best friends sometimes feel like family. We know that we will stick together regardless of where our individual paths lead.

We may be on the phone with our best friends every day, or we may not have spoken for a year—yet we know that our bond will be strong and immediate when we do connect. It ties us even when we are apart and draws us blissfully back into the warm refuge of each other's company when our paths bring us together again.

◇ ◇ ◇

SANCTIFY YOUR HOME
MAKING YOUR HOME A SANCTUARY

More than just somewhere to live, a home is a sanctuary, a place of refuge where serenity awaits. As well as a safe, nurturing space for the body, a home is a shrine for the spirit. We do much to make our homes comfortable and tranquil for ourselves and our families. We want to make them inviting to our friends as well. We can also reach out beyond our walls to send that tranquility out to the world, which so desperately needs love and compassion. Imagine transmitting healing energy that can transform lives without even leaving the comfort of your living room.

To create an environment from which to send loving light outward, start by going *inward*. Take care that your own body is well nurtured physically and spiritually with prayer, meditation, exercise, and good nutrition. Keeping a clean and tidy house honors the sanctity of your home, but beyond surface neatness, it is important to cleanse *regularly* as well.

Apply the spiritual principles of feng shui or vastu to create harmony in every room of your home. Open windows to let in fresh air and sunshine. Clear stagnant energy by smudging with sage or incense, drumming, and/or clapping.

Ask for a blessing on your home through prayer or meditation. Try the following:

In a quiet place, breathe in calmness and center yourself. Begin to focus on a small golden ball of light in front of your navel. Cup your hands around it and feel its warmth spread through your fingers, up your arms, radiating throughout your body. Imagine the ball of light growing in your hands, and open them to accommodate it. As it continues to grow, stretch your arms out wider until the golden ball overflows, spilling loving light all over the room. Now watch the light spread throughout your house, pouring out the doors and windows to your garden and into your neighborhood. See the light flow like lava until the whole earth is engulfed in a golden glow of peace and love.

Breathe deeply to return to your space, letting the glow continue to radiate loving energy to all. Allow yourself to bask in the light, and know that your home is a sanctuary for all who enter and even those beyond its physical boundaries.

◇ ◇ ◇

A SOFTER TOUCH
APPLY GENTLENESS TO EVERYTHING

Throughout life we must cope with blockages that impede our forward momentum. Whether these obstacles are of a personal, professional, or social nature, our first instinct may be to push against the obstruction. The simplest way to ease resistance, however, is to approach it gently, with a soft manner and kind intentions. Struggle and strife can find no foothold when confronted with mildness, because conflict can only exist when fed by two opposing forces. So many areas of our lives can benefit from the application of gentleness, the beauty of which lies in its multifaceted nature: It is part love, part compassion, part patience, part understanding, and part respect for others. When we move through life gently as a matter of course, we naturally attract these wonderful elements into our experience.

This does not mean that gentle people are by nature passive or meek. Rather, their copious inner power is manifested in their tenderness and their choice to move with the flow of the universe instead of against it. You can make use of gentleness in your own life by applying it in situations where you feel challenged by your circumstances or by people in your environment. As you move forward gently, the energy pervading your life will likely shift and, consequently, the blockages before you will vanish.

Cooperation progresses smoothly when approached gently because all parties involved feel confident that their needs will be met. And quarrels are easily quelled with gentleness because the dualistic concept of losing and winning are made moot by our willingness to exercise infinite patience with those whose values differ from our own.

Gentleness must be *practiced,* since you are inadvertently encouraged to act competitive in certain phases of your life. At first, your established habits may make being truly gentle challenging. After a time, if you commit to consciously applying gentleness to all areas of your life, whether by collaborating rather than competing or yielding graciously to the impassable roadblocks in your path in order to seek a new one, you will find that you begin to act in this way habitually. Your patterns of thought and behavior become more peaceful, and you will discover that you encounter far less insurmountable resistance on your individual journey.

◇ ◇ ◇

ABOVE THE CLOUDS

THE SUN IS ALWAYS SHINING

There are times when gloom or darkness causes us to momentarily lose sight of the light. It is on these occasions that the thought of the sun can help us. Its warm, glowing rays brighten even our thoughts, and it is good to remember that despite appearances, it is shining right now. We may not always be able to see it if clouds block our view, but they are only filtering its light temporarily. If darkness has fallen, we know that the sun is still shining at this very moment somewhere not too far away, and it is only a matter of time before it will cast its rays on us again.

When we remember that the sun is shining, we know that things are still in motion in the universe. Even if life feels as if it is at a standstill, sometimes all we need to do is have faith and wait for the time when everything is in its perfect place. Or we can choose to follow the cues of the sun and continue doing our work and shining our light even when we do not yet see results. In doing so, we exercise our patience, making sure that we are prepared when opportunity knocks and that all other elements are in their right and perfect places.

The sun also reminds us that our own shining truth is never extinguished. Our light is within us at all times, no matter what else occurs around us. Although the sun gives us daily proof of its existence, sometimes our belief in our own radiance requires more time. If we think back, however, we can find moments when it showed itself and trust that we will see it again. Like the sun, our light is the energy that connects us to the movements of the universe and the cycles of life; and it is present at all times, whether we feel its glow or not.

◇ ◇ ◇

APPROACHING CHANGE
WITH REVERENCE
THE WISDOM OF FEAR

Anything worth doing always has some fear attached to it. For example, having a baby, getting married, or changing careers — all of these life changes can bring up deep worries. It helps to remember that this type of fear is good. It is your way of questioning whether you really want the new life these changes will bring. It is also a potent reminder that releasing and grieving for the past is a necessary part of moving into the new.

Fear has a way of throwing us off balance, making us feel uncertain and insecure, but it is not meant to discourage us. Its purpose is to notify us that we are at the edge of our comfort zone, poised in between our old life and a new one. Whenever we face our fear, we overcome an inner obstacle and move into novel and life-enhancing territory, both inside and out.

The more we learn to respect fear and even welcome it, the more we will be able to hear its wisdom, which lets us know that the time has come to move forward — or not. While "comfort with fear" is a contradiction in terms, we can learn to honor our fear, recognizing its arrival, listening to its intelligence, and respecting it as a harbinger of transformation. Indeed, it informs us that the change we are contemplating is significant, enabling us to approach it with the proper reverence.

You might wish to converse with your fear, plumbing its depths for a greater understanding of the change you are making. You could do this by sitting quietly in meditation and listening or by journaling. Writing down whatever comes up — your worries, sadness, excitement, and hopes — is a great way to learn about yourself through the vehicle of fear and to remember that this emotion almost always comes alongside anything worth doing in your life.

◇ ◇ ◇

AN INVITATION TO LOVE
ANGEL MEDITATION

Although your host of spirit guides encompasses many diverse beings, all of which willingly watch over you, meditating with angels can be a uniquely insightful experience. These heavenly helpers stationed at your side are both powerful and knowledgeable. They possess a limitless understanding of your needs and desires, your strengths and weaknesses, and your purpose. However, angels take an active part in your life only when invited to do so. Meditation allows you to make contact with them and lovingly request that they participate actively in your day-to-day life.

To begin, retreat to a solitary place where you will not be distracted by any concerns. Incense and candlelight may aid you in achieving a meditative state but are not necessary. Display an image of an angel, angel statue, or another item symbolizing these beings before you focus your thoughts.

Sit comfortably, breathe deeply, and let yourself relax. When you feel peaceful, invite your angels from the highest of light to sit with you as you meditate. Mentally repeat your request, reiterating that this time together is important to you. Then, in your mind's eye, visualize a bright white light floating above you. As you breathe, draw it first into the crown of your head and then into the whole of your physical self. Allow this light to spread through your arms and hands, your core, and your lower body. Repeat this integration of illumination, this time with a violet light.

Once again, ask your angels to be with you. Let the stillness surrounding you enter your soul, and open your heart to your angelic guides. If they wish to communicate a message, they will do so now. Allow them to wrap their wings around you and infuse you with their bountiful love. Breathe them in just as you did the light.

As the meditation draws to a close, you may feel a presence, fluttering wings, or billowing fabric; or you may see an angel in your mind's eye. Thank heaven for providing you with love and light and being with you as you meditated. If you do not sense or feel anything, there is no cause for worry — you can be certain your angels are with you.

Do not be surprised if you start to see signs throughout the day that your angels are close by (a feather at your doorstep, perhaps). As you practice this meditation, you will become increasingly adept at recognizing when they are near and sensing their presence.

◇ ◇ ◇

BURNING BRIGHTLY
ALLOWING YOUR SOUL TO SHINE

At times we have all wanted to crawl under a rock and hide from the world. We may have preferred to be invisible rather than let other people see us or notice that we exist. This desire not to be seen often happens when we are feeling very hurt, angry, or simply weary of the world. And while we may console ourselves with the defense that we are shy, introverted, or solitary, we could actually be hiding.

When we make believe we are invisible, we may think that no one sees us — even though, truthfully, we are only hiding from ourselves. And while we may try to live life as inconspicuously as possible, we only succeed in becoming *more* conspicuous because people cannot help but notice that we are trying to conceal our light. None of us are meant to hide; each one of us radiates a unique brilliance that is meant to illuminate the world. When we try to dim our light, we diminish the natural radiance of the universe, and we deprive the people around us of the unique gifts and talents that we are here to share.

Stepping out of the wings and letting our light shine is actually a way to serve the planet. We each have a responsibility to contribute to our community, and we do this when we let ourselves be seen. It does no one any good when we try to hide. We are all beings of light, and we are here to illuminate the way for each other. When we let ourselves shine, we become a bright mirror through which others can see their own reflected brilliance, and they cannot help but want to shine, also.

Cast your light out into the world, bless those around you by sharing your gifts, and watch the universe glow.

◇ ◇ ◇

WRITING WITH AN ATTITUDE OF GRATITUDE
KEEPING A "GRATEFUL" JOURNAL

Some days it is easier to be appreciative of life than others, but if you really take note, there is *always* something to be grateful for. It is important to be grateful, and by acknowledging life's blessings, you actually invite more good things into your life.

Keeping a gratitude journal can remind you of all the things you have to be thankful for. Find an attractive blank book, or make one yourself. You can even use an ordinary notebook. Make your journal colorful by writing with different-colored pens. Or pick one shade for each category of appreciation: pink for pretty sights, yellow for friends . . . even green for prosperity.

You can journal daily, weekly, or monthly, but it is best to be consistent. Mark the date and write down what you are grateful for, why, and the circumstances that created the gratitude. The journal will become a chronicle of your feelings and experiences. It is fun to read your own writing from the past, and journaling keeps you in appreciation mode, reminding you of all the things that make you happy.

If you write on a daily basis, you can set a goal for yourself of recording a specific number of things to be thankful for each day. As you get into the habit of counting your blessings, you may soon find that you start being appreciative of so much more. You can set a new target number or just go wild and write as many things as you can think of. Most of us have myriad reasons to be grateful, and it is easy to find the obvious. However, after a few days, you begin to get past the mundane — such as food, shelter, and clothing — and begin to appreciate many other things in life. When you start to look for them, you will find that you are rewarded with countless gifts of gratitude. People will enter your life for just a moment and leave you with a gem of kindness or just a simple smile.

Pass the gratitude attitude along by offering gifts of journals to your family and friends to record *their* thankfulness. You can start them off by sharing what *you* appreciate about them. Describe what they have given you, what you have observed about them, and what you wish for them. Being appreciated is one of the best gifts you can bestow on someone. Write it down and it is lasting.

◇ ◇ ◇

INTERTWINED FATES
WE ARE ALL CONNECTED

There are times when we may feel disconnected from the world. Our actions can seem to be of no major consequence, and we may feel as if we exist in our own vacuum. The truth is that our simplest thought or deed — the decisions we make each day and how we see and relate to the world — can be incredibly significant and have a profound impact on the lives of those around us, as well as the world at large.

The earth, and everything on it, is bound by an invisible connection between humans, animals, plants, the air, the water, and the soil. Insignificant actions on your part, whether positive or negative, can have an impact on people and environments that seem entirely separate from your personal realm of existence. Staying conscious of the interconnection between all things can help you think of your choices and your life in terms of the broader effect you may be creating.

Think of buying a wooden stool: The material it is made of was once part of a tree, which was part of a forest. A person was paid to fell the tree, another to cut the wood, and yet another to build the stool. Their income may have had a positive effect on their families, just as the loss of the tree may have had a negative impact on the forest or the animals that made it their home.

Likewise, an encouraging word to a young child about a special talent can influence him or her to develop this gift so that one day his or her inventions can change the lives of millions. A poem written to express oneself can make a stranger reading it online thousands of miles away feel less alone because there is someone else out there who feels exactly the way he or she does.

Staying conscious of your connection to all things can help you think of your choices in terms of their impact. You are powerful enough so that what you do and say can reverberate through the lives of people you may never meet. Recognizing that you are intimately connected with all things and understanding your power to affect the world can be the first steps on the road to living more consciously.

◇ ◇ ◇

REMEMBERING WHO WE ARE
BRAVE SPIRITS

Most of us are familiar with the idea that we are not human beings having spiritual experiences; instead, we are *spiritual* beings having *human* experiences. We hear this, and even though we may experience a resounding *Yes!* in our bodies, we may not take the time to really acknowledge the truth of this statement. Integrating this idea into how we view ourselves can broaden our sense of who we are and help us appreciate ourselves as brave spirits on an important mission to learn and grow here on Earth.

As spiritual beings, we are visitors in this physical realm. The fact that we came here and lost all memory of what happened to us before we were born is one of the many reasons why it takes so much courage for a soul to incarnate on Earth. This is why spiritual inquiry so often feels like a remembering—because it *is*. Recalling that we are spiritual beings is part of the work we are here on this planet to do.

When we operate from a place of remembering, we tap into the wisdom that our spirit accumulated even before we stepped into this lifetime. Recollecting who we are can give us the patience to persevere when we become overwhelmed or frustrated. It can lend us the courage to work through the most daunting challenges and help us trust the ancient wisdom that we carry offered to us by our intuition.

We have chosen to be on Earth because there is something we want to learn that can only happen by inhabiting a body. Some of us are here to repay a debt, gain knowledge of love, or teach forgiveness. Most of us are here for a combination of reasons. We carry this information in our souls; all we have to do is remember.

As you go through your journey, try not to forget how brave you are in being here now. Honor yourself.

◇ ◇ ◇

AN EMPTY VESSEL
CAN BE FILLED
THE POWER OF NOT KNOWING

There is wisdom in not knowing, and it is a wise person who can say "I don't know." There are many types of wisdom — from intellectual to emotional to physical. Even purported experts in their fields do not know *all* there is to know about mathematics, yoga, literature, psychology, or art. It is a true master who professes ignorance, for only an empty vessel can be filled.

There are many things in life that we do not know, and many we may have no interest in finding out about. There is freedom in saying "I don't know." When we admit this, we can then open ourselves up to the opportunity to learn — and there is power in that. We cannot possibly know *everything*. And when we think we do, we limit ourselves from growing and learning more. People who can own up to not knowing tend to be more intellectually and emotionally confident than those who pretend to know it all. They are also likely to be more comfortable with who they are and not feel the need to bluff or cover up any perceived ignorance. People can actually end up appearing more foolish when they act as if they have knowledge that they do not.

We would be well advised to respect people who freely admit when they do not know something — they are being honest with us and with themselves. And we, too, should feel no shame in saying "I don't know." In doing so, we open ourselves up to the unknown. We can then discover what lies beyond our current levels of understanding. It is the wise person in life who responds to questions with a question and inspires the pursuit of internal answers with a funny face, a shrug, and a comical "I don't know."

◇ ◇ ◇

ELEGANT BLESSINGS
LIVING A LIFE OF GRACE

Grace exists inside and around all of us. It is our inner beauty that radiates outward, touching everyone we meet. It is that unseen hand that comes from the divine, raising us up when we most need it. Living in a state of grace is not based on worthiness; nor is it earned through good deeds, ritual, or sacrifice. Rather, it is an unearned favor, freely bestowed and available to all, one that is inherent in our birthright. All we must do is open our eyes to its presence and we will find and experience it everywhere.

Grace is in the rain bringing relief to drought-ridden farms, and the unexpected lead for the perfect job opportunity that comes from a stranger. It is what happens to someone when they miraculously escape injury; it is even the simple events that happen to us that we call "good luck" — when we do not get a parking ticket after our meter has expired, for instance. Grace resides in the love between two people, the gift or check that comes unexpectedly in the mail, the cozy comforts that make up a home, and the acts of forgiveness we bestow upon others. It is grace that moves us to go out of our way to help a stranger. Grace is the state we are in when we are doing nothing but just being who we are.

When we accept that we always exist in this state, we are able to live our lives more *graciously*. Knowing we are "graced" lends us hope, makes us more giving, and allows us to trust that we are taken care of even when we are going through difficult times. Grace is our benevolence of heart and our generosity of spirit. It is unconditional love and the beauty that is our humanity. When we know that we are blessed with grace, we cannot help but want to live our lives in harmony.

◇ ◇ ◇

AFTERWORD

It is my sincere hope that reading these passages has brought about a shift in your life. Making change happen in your life can be joyful and exciting, and it can also be scary. Be gentle with yourself as you allow the words in these pages to fill your heart and soul. Be good to yourself and take the time you need to process the information. More important, congratulate yourself for being a courageous and brave spirit living on planet Earth. Remember your beauty — you are a beautiful being of light.

ACKNOWLEDGMENTS

I would like to thank:

- Scott Blum, my husband and DailyOM co-founder

- My editorial staff for taking the journey with me: Christa Terry, Malayna Weeratunga, Mick Kubiak, Margaret Schultze, and Anna Skinner

And a special thanks to our DailyOM staff and supporters.

— Madisyn

◇ ◇ ◇

ABOUT DAILYOM

DailyOM features a universal approach to holistic living for the mind, body, and spirit and supports people who want to live a conscious lifestyle. You can find more DailyOM, register for a free daily inspirational newsletter, or find products and gift items that can help you on your journey of healing and awareness on the DailyOM Website: **www.dailyom.com**.

ABOUT MADISYN TAYLOR

Madisyn Taylor is the co-founder and editor-in-chief of DailyOM and is responsible for all the content on its Website. She is also the founder and head of product development for the successful aromatherapy and spiritual-jewelry line named Madisyn Taylor. Additionally, Madisyn has several years' experience in personal development and alternative-healing methodologies. When not writing or developing products, Madisyn can be found in her garden playing with her cat, Zoe, and being at one with nature. She also enjoys journaling, meditating, and taking walks with her husband in the forest near their home in Ashland, Oregon.

◇ ◇ ◇

We hope you enjoyed this Hay House book. If you'd like to receive our online catalog featuring additional information on Hay House books and products, or if you'd like to find out more about the Hay Foundation, please contact:

Hay House, Inc.
P.O. Box 5100
Carlsbad, CA 92018-5100

(760) 431-7695 or **(800) 654-5126**
(760) 431-6948 (fax) or **(800) 650-5115 (fax)**
www.hayhouse.com® • **www.hayfoundation.org**

◆

Published and distributed in Australia by: Hay House Australia Pty. Ltd., 18/36 Ralph St., Alexandria NSW 2015 • *Phone:* 612-9669-4299 *Fax:* 612-9669-4144 • www.hayhouse.com.au

Published and distributed in the United Kingdom by: Hay House UK, Ltd., 292B Kensal Rd., London W10 5BE • *Phone:* 44-20-8962-1230 *Fax:* 44-20-8962-1239 • www.hayhouse.co.uk

Published and distributed in the Republic of South Africa by: Hay House SA (Pty), Ltd., P.O. Box 990, Witkoppen 2068 • *Phone/Fax:* 27-11-467-8904 • info@hayhouse.co.za • www.hayhouse.co.za

Published in India by: Hay House Publishers India, Muskaan Complex, Plot No. 3, B-2, Vasant Kunj, New Delhi 110 070 • *Phone:* 91-11-4176-1620 *Fax:* 91-11-4176-1630 • www.hayhouse.co.in

Distributed in Canada by: Raincoast, 9050 Shaughnessy St., Vancouver, B.C. V6P 6E5 • *Phone:* (604) 323-7100 • *Fax:* (604) 323-2600 www.raincoast.com

◆

<u>**Take Your Soul on a Vacation**</u>

Visit **www.HealYourLife.com®** to regroup, recharge, and reconnect with your own magnificence. Featuring blogs, mind-body-spirit news, and life-changing wisdom from Louise Hay and friends.

Visit **www.HealYourLife.com** today!